The Woodwright's Shop

The Woodwright's Shop

A Practical Guide to Traditional
Woodcraft / by Roy Underhill

The University of North Carolina Press / Chapel Hill

© 1981 The University of North Carolina Press

All rights reserved

Manufactured in the United States of America

Library of Congress Cataloging in Publication Data
Underhill, Roy.
    The woodwright's shop.

    Includes index.
    1. Woodwork.   2. Woodworking tools.   3. Wood-
work—History—19th century.   4. Woodworking tools—
History—19th century.   I. Title.
TT180.U47   684'.082   81-2960
ISBN 0-8078-1484-9   AACR2
ISBN 0-8078-4082-3 (pbk.)

PHOTO CREDITS
Daniel Ellison: 182, 193–96
Lance Richardson: 45, 46(b, c), 47(a), 49–51, 106,
110–13, 116, 117
Jim Bullock: 81
all others by R. E. U.

For my mother and father

Contents

Thanks

Living and working in three different centuries can keep you very busy—if not totally confused—and without a lot of help it would be impossible.

Among friends and colleagues in eighteenth-century Williamsburg, I am particularly indebted to Earl Soles, director of the Crafts Department, for his patience and assistance while I was working on this book and to apprentices Mark Berninghausen and Ed Smith for running the carpenters' yard in my absence. My colonial comrades, master blacksmith Peter Ross and lady Claire Mehalick, have been kind and generous sources of encouragement and inspiration. Burke Davis has been an enthusiastic mentor in helping me deal with the new business of books and publishing.

The nineteenth-century world of my old shop where this book takes place owes its existence to the staff and friends of West Point Mill on the Eno. Among the dozen stalwarts who helped to build the shop was Dan Ellison, whose six photos of raising the shop appear in the last chapter. Jacquie Fehon, director of archaeology for the state of North Carolina, gave this manuscript its first going over.

The twentieth-century production of "The Woodwright's Shop" for television was made a true pleasure by producer-director Geary Morton, executive producer Bobby Royster, publicist Alvin Hall, and the rest of the staff of the University of North Carolina Center for Public Television. On the other side of town, at the University of North Carolina Press, David Perry, editor, and Rich Hendel, designer, have wrought a similar transformation with my words and photographs.

It's a privilege to be able to work seriously in this field. For this I must credit the encouragement received from Fred White of the School of Forestry at Duke University and Ed Hawes of Sangamon State University. Thanks to you both.

Jane, you put up with this nonsense long enough for me to finish it. Thanks be to all of you—it's done.

The Woodwright's Shop

Introduction

They were friends, as only a craftsman can be, with
timber and iron. The grain of the wood told secrets to them.
—George Sturt, *The Wheelwright's Shop* (1923)

I teach traditional hand-tool wood-working—how to start with a tree and an axe and make one thing after another until you have a house and everything in it. The satisfactions of this work are immediate and personal. You find the tree, fell it, shape the wood, and join it together. The mistakes and successes, the accidents and discoveries are between you and the tree.

We have spent millennia devising ways to avoid this sort of physical work, and yet we always return to it. It is a part of us. Hardwood trees and humans appeared on the planet at about the same time, and the two of us have grown together. The origins of this relationship reach beyond tradition into instinct, all the way back to the prehuman necessity for correctly judging the strength of the next tree branch before swinging to it. It's what used to be known as common sense, and it's what this book is about.

The tools of the woodworker's trade range from the grinding rock and froe club to the great-wheel lathe and the skew-mouthed panel-raising plane. A large part of this book is about making your own tools to work with. The tools are essential; their grace and deliberateness make your hand reach out to them— lightning rods to ground the creative spark.

This sort of handwork may appear comparatively benign, but even without our fossil fuels we are powerful and persistent creatures. The land around the Mediterranean was made into a desert not by power equipment but by bronze axes and domestic goats. And although I have never seen anyone strangle himself by getting his necktie caught while turning on a foot-powered lathe, I have seen a man very nearly split his foot in half with the mis-directed blow of a felling axe. The responsibility remains very real.

In *The Woodwright's Shop* I have tried to show you some of the ways I work. I change my technique all the time to match new materials, designs, tools, and moods. Sometimes I need to work fast and will knock out a finished chair every day for a week or make a rake an hour until I have enough to take to market. Thankfully, there are other times when I can work slowly and figure out new ways of working as I go along. I work by eye and by feel. This book reflects the way I work; I am less concerned with numbers and measurements than I am with promoting experience and the development of confidence in your senses.

Each chapter leads into the next in a progression of tools and techniques. If you make everything in this book, you will have touched on most of the essential techniques of hand woodworking. Since you will be using such a broad range of skills, you can expect things to go wrong occasionally. You need to learn from mistakes, but you must also learn to protect yourself from getting discouraged. If something doesn't work out and you feel bad about it, go immediately and do something else that you can accomplish easily. Rub down your wooden planes with linseed oil or hone your axe to a razor edge. Nothing succeeds like success—and your planes will always be well oiled. I know mine are.

Chapter 1. Trees

The best and the poorest grow together, even of the
same varieties. . . . It doesn't seem to be locality so much as
it is the individuality of the tree itself. It is something I
cannot explain.
—W. G. Shepard in *Practical Carriage Building* (1892)

Like an old recipe for rabbit stew that begins "first you catch a rabbit," so in traditional country woodworking you first must find and fell a suitable tree. Even craftsmen who relied on others to fell the timber often bought their wood still in the round log. Before anything else, then, you need to be able to recognize the right tree when you see it, not only by the characteristics common to its particular species, like the toughness of elm, which suits it so well for wheel hubs, but also by the looks of the individual tree.

Reading the Bark

Wood forms in a layer of rapidly dividing cells called the cambium, which is located just inside the inner bark. As the tree grows, this layer produces wood to the inside and bark (essentially) to the outside. Since both bark and wood are produced in the same place, some of the characteristics of the wood can be inferred from the appearance of the bark. If the furrows in the bark spiral up the tree, the wood probably does the same. Places where the bark has healed over old branches are easily seen; they, of course, mean knots down in the wood. Soft bark with long flakes is a good indicator of slow growth and tight-grained wood. Daily experience from working with trees from the forests and hedgerows that I see every day has taught me what to look for. This is the only way that you can come to know what to expect from the trees in your particular part of the forest. Look at your trees and see what their outsides tell

The bark of this white oak spirals up to the right. The wood inside will do the same.

The bark on this old dead red oak showed that it would split straight.

you about how they have grown. After a while, you'll be able to look at a tree and tell exactly what sort of chair, basket, or house it has within it.

Sapwood and Heartwood

When you chop into a tree as you fell it, notice how the color of the outer few inches of wood is lighter than that further in. In some species the difference may be hard to spot. Only these outer few inches of lighter colored sapwood are alive and functioning; the darker interior wood is essentially dead, but provides the tree with mechanical support. The dividing line between the two is constantly moving outward as the tree grows because the older sapwood

to the inside is constantly turning into heartwood.

As the living cells of the sapwood "turn off" and become heartwood, they build up deposits of chemicals called extractives, which are resistant to fungi and insect attack. This passive defense against bugs and rot lasts after the tree is cut. The living sapwood of the tree, however, depends on active, biological resistance, an ability it loses when the tree is cut. This is why any sapwood left on a fence post will rot off long before the heartwood is affected; it can defend itself only when it is alive. This also explains how insects and decay that are able to overcome the passive resistance of the heartwood of a tree but not the active resistance of the living sapwood can completely hollow a tree out without killing it. This last trick is one that we humans have

yet to figure out. The properties of heartwood make it very useful to man, and the tree could go on living without it, but we have yet to discover how to get to it without killing the tree.

Changes

Traditional country woodworking means working with the wood from a living tree. Beyond changing the shape of the wood from the tree, the woodworker also changes its en-

The heartwood of the maple log on the left was eaten out while the tree was still alive and growing. The sapwood of the red oak on the right decayed when the tree died, but its heartwood is still sound.

color, dimensions, and a host of other properties. This is what makes wood "alive." A large part of working with wood is the ability to anticipate and work with these changes.

Strength

A constant source of amazement to the casual observer is the ease and speed with which traditional wood-workers are able to shape their materials. Of course, they know how to use their tools, but more important, they are often working in freshly cut wood. When wood has been freshly cut and is soft and swollen with water, it chops easier, splits easier, bends easier, and saws easier than it does when it dries out.

Green wood does have its drawbacks, however. An article made of wood that is still green is easily broken if it is not allowed to dry before being used. A wooden beam placed in a building before it has had a chance to dry out will often sag under its own weight and dry with the sag in it. The message here is shape the wood while it is green and use it when it has dried. As the wood dries out, its weight decreases and its strength and stiffness increase.

Dimensional Changes

If the strength of wood were all that changed with changes in its moisture content, working with wood would be a lot simpler. But the structure of wood is such that as it dries, it shrinks, and as it takes on water, it swells. Fit a handle of green wood into the head of an axe, and it will come flying off within a week. Drive a peg of dry wood into a hole drilled into rock and pour water on it, and it will split the stone. This swelling

The post-seasoning distortion of wood shaped while green. The red-oak disk has cracked or checked to relieve the stress caused by the shrinkage in circumference being twice as great as the radial shrinkage. The sycamore bowl is now humped on the end-grain sides. The pine board begins to cup slightly near the heart, and the rectangle of the red-oak beam has become lopsided.

vironment. Life inside a tree is very wet; living wood is up to two-thirds water by weight. Once taken down and exposed, however, wood starts drying out and continues drying until it reaches an equilibrium with the relative humidity of its new environment. In wood left outside under cover (air drying), the moisture content drops slowly until it is about one-sixth water by weight. This drying process is known as "seasoning."

But it doesn't stop there. Fully seasoned wood is at peace with its surroundings only insofar as those surroundings remain constant. If the humidity changes, the wood will absorb or release moisture until it is again in balance. Wood that has been kept in a dry house will take on additional water from the air if it is moved to a damp garage. Firewood from the garage will lose moisture when brought into the house. Water in wood affects its weight, strength, and shrinking is why some wooden doors stick in the summer and open up cracks in the winter. The wood is constantly moving in response to changes in the humidity.

But there's more to this simple swelling and shrinking. Wood also swells and shrinks differently in different directions. Along the length of the grain, change is negligible. A 4-foot length of green firewood will still be 4 feet long when it dries. In the two transverse directions—across the grain—however, the change is quite significant and must be allowed for. In the radial plane (across the growth rings) the shrinkage from green to air dried is about 3 percent. In the tangential plane (parallel to the growth rings) shrinkage is twice what it is radially. This is why a disk sawed off the end of a log will crack open on its radius as it dries. The tangential shrinkage is so much greater than the radial shrinkage that cracking is the only way for the circumference to contract. This uneven shrinkage also causes the distortion of sawn lumber and other articles made from green wood. As long as the weather keeps changing, this motion never stops. You have to learn to anticipate its effects. Design with this potential for change in mind.

Directional Strength

The strength of wood also varies with the direction of the grain. A block of wood stood on end can be split with one blow of the axe. Many strokes would be needed to cut through the same piece of wood laid flat so that the blows cut across the grain. This resistance to splitting (tension failure) is different from what happens when the wood is hit with the flat poll of the axe. In this case the wood is under compres-

sion. A blow that leaves the end grain undented will easily smash in the side of the log. This is why the business end of a wooden mallet is end grain.

The shear resistance of wood also varies with the direction of the grain. Imagine clamping a 2-inch cube of wood halfway down in the jaws of a vise and then trying to knock off the top half with a hammer. If you clamp the block so that the failure will be along the grain, this shouldn't be too difficult. If, however, you try it with the end grain of the block facing upward so that the shear would have to be across the grain, you may knock the vise off the bench.

These general characteristics of the way wood behaves have shaped the world we live in. A great part of the evolution of design has been dictated by the nature of this material. We shape and join our creations with this understanding.

The Trees

There is a right kind of wood for every job. The thousands of different species of woody plants that populate the earth all have their individual characteristics that we have discovered and learned to use to our advantage. We even use this shared knowledge in speaking about one another. Someone called "Old Hickory" is obviously quite a bit different from someone described as "willowy," but there are places for both—some situations call for toughness and some for grace.

Here are a few of the trees that I work with:

APPLE (*Malus sp.*). This is the tree that taught Sir Isaac Newton about gravity. Apple and pear wood are excellent for making wooden

The smooth, platy bark of apple trees is often perforated by yellow-bellied sapsuckers.

machine parts, especially wooden screws and nuts. The wood takes a deep polish; it is often used in decorative carving and tool handles. Fruit wood like this can often be obtained in large quantities in orchard country following ice storms.

ASH (*Fraxinus sp.*). Ash and hickory go together. Although ash is somewhat less tough and less shock resistant than hickory, it is lighter and more versatile. Because of its excellent bending characteristics, it is widely used for making hay forks, bent scythe handles, and bentwood chairs. Straight grained and readily shaped by cleaving, it seasons well and holds its shape when dry. It is preferred for making shovel handles and sporting equipment such as bats and oars because of its toughness and strength and its ability to stay smooth under constant rubbing. A superior wood for wheel and wagon work, but low in resistance to decay.

BEECH (*Fagus grandifolia*). Beech wood is difficult to season without excessive checking and distortion, but once dried, its strength and ability to wear smoothly make it the standard for wooden plane bodies. It is low in decay resistance and not an easy wood to work with hand tools, but it turns well on a lathe and can be readily bent after steaming. These qualities suit it well for use in chair manufacture. The beech forests in Britain once sheltered itinerant woodturners, called "chair bodgers," who cleft beech blanks and shaped them on their spring-pole lathes into legs for Windsor chairs.

BIRCH (*Betula sp.*). Birch wood shares many characteristics with hard maple. It is heavy, hard, strong, and stiff. Its shock resistance and close grain make it valuable as a commercial furniture wood. Birch is somewhat difficult to work with hand tools and has low resistance to decay. Because it turns well and takes

a high polish, it is used extensively for domestic woodenware such as plates, bowls, and spoons. These qualities also suit it well for use as bobbins, spools, clothespins, and toothpicks. Shrinkage during seasoning is considerable.

BLACK CHERRY (*Prunus serotina*). Black- or wild-cherry trees do not like competition for sunlight from other trees. For this reason they are usually found in old openings in the forest or along fence rows where birds have paused after eating the somewhat bitter fruit. The wood resists warping and splitting during seasoning. After seasoning, it remains exceptionally stable. The beauty of the reddish brown wood, along with its stability and strength, makes it prized for high-quality work in furniture, scientific instruments, and sculpture.

BLACK LOCUST (*Robinia pseudo-acacia*). The yellow, dense, coarse-

grained wood of black locust is heavy, very hard, and stiff. Its strength and superb resistance to decay make it valuable for pole barns and sills. Its low shrinkage during seasoning and its general dimensional stability suit it well for such uses as pegs for timber-frame buildings and pins for glass insulators on power lines. Locust splits well and makes excellent fence posts and rails. It is good for machinery parts and any job that requires exceptional strength. Not the easiest wood to work, but one that will last.

BLACK WALNUT (*Juglans nigra*). Walnut is unquestionably the most gratifying wood to work with hand tools. The deep brown wood with occasional streaks of purple is our finest domestic cabinet stock. Straight-grained walnut can be readily split into the rough blanks for further shaping. Very resistant to rot, it has been used for posts and pilings. Walnut trees are slow growing, hence

The compound leaves of ash trees (here are four) grow in opposite pairs from the twig. Hickory leaves are similar but are staggered or alternate as they come from the twig.

Beech leaves have distinct, parallel veins.

Birches love moist soil. This river birch shows rough, papery bark.

their current scarcity. Finding a
walnut tree in the forest often
indicates an old house site. The
punky white sapwood on a fallen log
near old foundations may conceal a
beautiful treasure within.

CHESTNUT (*Castanea dentata*). Once
an important and valuable contribu-
tor to the local economy, chestnut
has largely been killed off by a
fungus blight of European origin that
entered this country in 1909. The
wood is coarse grained and has a
beautiful brown color that deepens
with age. It is light, soft, and rather
weak, but very durable in contact
with the soil. Many fields are still
fenced with rails that were split over
a hundred years ago. The bleached
bones of chestnut trees killed by the
blight are often found in the forests,
sometimes with living sprout growth
coming from the stump.

DOGWOOD (*Cornus florida*). Dogwood is dense, hard, strong, and very

*The compound leaves, spiny twigs, and rough dark brown bark make black locust
easy to spot.*

*Black-cherry bark is smooth and glossy
when young, but becomes rough and platy
with age.*

*The compound leaves of black walnut
have from fifteen to twenty-three leaflets.*

*A dead tree in the woods that has not
begun to decay may be a chestnut. The
sapwood will be thin and white, the
heartwood coarse and brown.*

close grained. Because it responds to wear by becoming even smoother, it is used for industrial weaving shuttles and wooden machinery bearings. It is also an excellent choice for turned items like spools, pulleys, and mallet heads. Dogwood is heavy and difficult to split; it makes superior wedges and tool handles.

EASTERN RED CEDAR (*Juniperus virginiana*). The contrast between the bright red heartwood and the white sapwood makes red cedar a hard one to miss. The heartwood is highly rot resistant and moderately hard, but weak in bending. The fragrance of the wood is quite pleasing and reputed to be moth repellent. It has good seasoning characteristics and is quite stable. The wood is straight grained and splits well, but is generally knotty and available only in small sizes. In clear pieces it works very easily with hand tools.

ELM (*Ulmus sp.*). Elm is exceedingly difficult to split. For this reason it is a primary choice for the hubs for wagon wheels or in any situation where its interlocked grain can be used to advantage. It is not easy to work with and is moderately weak, but it bends readily. Elm is normally not very resistant to decay, but when exposed to constant dampness, it lasts indefinitely. Hence, it was the customary material for wooden water pipes and pumps. Elm turns well on a lathe and makes excellent bowls and plates. An elm stump is the traditional woodworker's chopping block and the pedestal for the blacksmith's anvil.

HACKBERRY (*Celtis occidentalis*). Hackberry, as well as its cousin sugarberry, seems to have an identity problem. When its grain is interlocked and tough, it is sold at sawmills as elm. When the grain is straight, they sell it as ash. It is an outstandingly average wood in

weight, hardness, and decay resistance. This tree is found throughout the country, so if you can't locate the wood you want, you might try hackberry.

HICKORY (*Carya sp.*). Nothing beats hickory in its combination of exceptional strength, hardness, toughness, and resiliency. The premier wood for axe handles and other applications that call for superior shock resistance, it is also used in making wheel spokes and the undercarriages for wagons. Hickory must be very carefully seasoned; it shrinks a great deal and is subject to checking and warping. Usually straight grained, it splits well when green. Its value as firewood has been long appreciated. Hickory has low resistance to decay.

HORNBEAM (*Carpinus caroliniana*). The white wood of hornbeam is very tough, close grained, heavy, and strong. Its toughness is echoed in its alternate common name—ironwood.

Dogwood is easy to tell by its bark.

Red cedars against the sky look as though they were painted on porcelain with a sponge.

Elms have a distinctive urn shape when growing in the open.

The tree never grows very big, so its use is limited to such things as cogs in mill machinery, tool bodies, wear plates, handles, mallets, and wedges. It has a relatively low resistance to decay and is a difficult wood to split.

LINDEN OR BASSWOOD (*Tilia sp.*). Basswood, also known as lime in Britain, is the favorite of sculptors and wood-carvers because of its ease of working and even grain. This is the wood for cigar-store Indians, figureheads, and hewn bowls. It's lightweight and rather soft and weak, but it has good resistance to unwanted splitting. The inner bark of basswood trees can be used to make coarse rope and even cloth. Honeybees appreciate its flowers, which also make an excellent tea.

MAPLE (*Acer sp.*). The sugar or hard maple of the North is one of our leading furniture woods. Its strength and hardness and finishing qualities

have given it a place in almost every home. The uniform texture is easy to work with and makes it an excellent choice for flooring, butcher blocks, doors, and other jobs where hard use

Hickory leaves are compound and alternate on the twig. The bark appears interwoven.

is the rule. Since it turns well on a lathe, it is often used in chair making. Hard maple shrinks a great deal during seasoning. Variations in the grain, such as curly, or "bird's-

The leaflike bracts and fruit of the linden remain through the winter.

Hackberry bark is grey and covered with warts. The leaves are thin and papery.

Hornbeam limbs are small and grey and look like they have muscles.

Maple leaves need no introduction.

eye," maple, are highly decorative. Soft maple species such as red maple have many of the same uses as the harder species, except that they are unsuited for jobs in which extra hardness is necessary.

WHITE OAK (*Quercus Leucobalanus sp.*). White oak rivals walnut as the king of the woods. Its versatility is unmatched. White-oak timber is heavy, hard, and very strong. It will make an axe handle that is nearly the equal of hickory or ash. The pores of white oak are blocked with inclusions called tyloses that make it impervious to liquids. This, coupled with its strength, makes it the only choice for whiskey barrels. Moderately resistant to decay, it is a prime timber for ship building. When sawn or split on the radial plane, the surface is quite distinctive, with large patches of silver grain. It is a difficult wood to season successfully, but worth the effort.

RED OAK (*Quercus Erythrobalanus sp.*). The dozen or so major species of red oaks can usually be distinguished from those of the white-oak group by the presence of tiny bristles or spines on the tips of the pointed lobes of the leaves. Red-oak wood is heavy, hard, and stiff, but extremely porous. If the end of a stick of red oak is placed in a cup of water and air blown through the other end, bubbles will appear in the water. This is why you never hear of red-oak whiskey barrels. Red oak is usually straight grained and easy to work with. It is an excellent furniture and construction material, although it will quickly decay in contact with the soil.

OSAGE ORANGE (*Maclura pomifera*). An East Texas native, the Osage orange has been widely planted and can now be found throughout the country. The wood is bright yellow when first exposed, but soon turns

an orangish brown. Because of its resistance to rot, it is widely used for fence posts. Osage-orange wood is very strong, heavy, and hard; it is often used in place of black locust. Its flexibility makes it a popular wood for use in hunting bows, hence its other name, "bois d'arc," or bow wood. It splits straight and is a generally useful wood.

PERSIMMON (*Diospyros virginiana*). Persimmon wood is hard, strong, and very heavy. A member of the ebony family, it is occasionally stained black and used as a substitute wood in piano keys. Its primary use, however, is for making wooden golf-club heads and weaving shuttles. The wide sapwood is yellowish, often tinged with streaks of brown or black. It is a difficult wood to work with and shrinks considerably during seasoning, but its toughness and ability to stay smooth under friction suit it for many special uses.

Mature white oaks have a light-colored bark composed of shaggy plates. The leaves are lobed and smooth at the ends of the veins.

Red oaks have many different leaf forms, but almost all are spiny or bristled at the ends of the veins.

The bark of Osage orange is yellow-brown, the twigs are spiny, the leaves are dark green and glossy, and the fruit looks like grapefruits.

The fruit of the persimmon can be eaten as soon as it is well wrinkled; you don't have to wait for a frost.

SASSAFRAS (*Sassafras albidum*). Sassafras wood is soft, weak, and rather brittle, but it is quite resistant to decay. It splits straight, is easy to work, and smells wonderful. Often used for small-boat construction, fence posts, and foundation posts, it's also a good wood for making wooden pails and ox yokes. Although it is not a strong wood, it, like red mulberry, is occasionally used in oversized dimensions for making country chairs. Sassafras turns well on a lathe.

SOUTHERN YELLOW PINE (*Pinus sp.*). Compared with the soft or white pine, with its homogenous grain, southern yellow or hard pine has a distinct contrast in color and hardness between the early- and later-formed wood in the annual growth rings. The slow growth of the original virgin timber produced fine-grained, resinous, decay-resistant wood that can easily be distinguished from the lightweight, wide-ringed wood of second-growth stock. Southern yellow pine is well suited for use in building construction. Shrinkage during seasoning is moderately large, but the dry wood is relatively stable. One-inch-thick pine boards can air dry in as little as three weeks.

SYCAMORE (*Platanus occidentalis*). Sycamore, sometimes called button-wood, is a very fast growing tree, often reaching a diameter of 10 feet and a height of 150 feet. It decays rapidly in contact with the ground. In fact, huge hollow sycamore trees were the first homes for many pioneer families. The wood is somewhat difficult to split and moderately strong and hard. It turns well on a lathe and makes excellent food containers, as it imparts no taste or stain. It is an excellent wood for butcher blocks and industrial flooring. A good wood for steam-bent furniture and boxes.

WILLOW (*Salix sp.*). This is the tree that gave us the expression "clean as a whistle." In the spring the bright green bark of the growing twigs can be easily slipped off to make willow whistles, leaving the pure white wood beneath the new bark. Willow wood is soft, light, and very weak. Its light weight and the ease with which it can be shaped with hand tools make it ideal for artificial arms and legs. The charcoal made from willow wood was prized for making black powder. Willow trees love water and can often be found along stream banks. It decays rapidly in contact with the ground.

YELLOW POPLAR OR TULIP TREE (*Liriodendron tulipifera*). Yellow poplar is not a true poplar like cotton-

Persimmon bark is dark black and broken into blocks. The mature fruit is wrinkled and globular.

Sassafras leaves come in three styles: mittens, double-thumbed mittens, and no-thumbed mittens.

Hard yellow pines usually have two or three needles in each bunch. Soft pines have five.

wood or aspen, but is actually
a member of the magnolia family.
A fast-growing tree, yellow poplar
lends itself to a wide variety of uses.
The wood is soft and light, but

Sycamore bark is white and mottled with flaking grey-brown plates.

Willows love the water. The weeping varieties are hard to miss.

Tulip poplars have grey, smoothly furrowed bark on perfectly tapered cylindrical trunks. Both the leaves and the flowers resemble tulips in bloom.

moderately stiff. It is usually straight grained, clear of knots, and very easy to work with hand tools. The sapwood is white and may make up a large percentage of younger trees. The heartwood ranges from a light green to a deep purple. Poplar is an easy wood to season and stays in place when dry. It is a favorite wood for wooden bowls, shovels, and hewn construction timbers, but it also decays rapidly in contact with the ground.

The "revenge oak" had stood for 120 years between the river and the road to the mill. A windstorm had taken it down, so that it had fallen up across the road, which is unusual. Most waterside trees branch out heaviest into the clear space over the water, where there is no competition for sunlight. This makes these trees heavier on the water side; which is why beavers have such good luck in getting them to fall into their ponds. This one, however, had fallen away from the water and was lying on a slight uphill rise. Its base was a huge root wad of rock and clay, at least 6 feet to its highest point. Someone had already cut away the branches down to the 3-foot-diameter main trunk. This was left, clear and straight, about 14 feet long.

My brother, Tom, and I went to work on it, cutting it up into 2-foot lengths for shingle bolts. As we finished sawing off a section, we split it down into pieces that were light enough to carry the quarter mile back to the shop.

We started at the top end and worked our way down to the uprooted base. We had just about finished splitting up the fourth section when suddenly I had a sense of massive motion close behind me. Years of dodging falling trees made my muscles tense up. I quickly looked up at Tom, who was standing dumbstruck, gaping at something awesome happening directly behind me. That was all I needed to see, and I jumped as far as I could away from whatever it was. I landed off to the side in a bank of nettles just as the water jug, my axe, and the crosscut saw splashed into the middle of the river. I had last seen those items sitting where I had left them, on top of the uncut remainder of the oak—the same oak that was now standing upright in its former position. Apparently, after we had cut off so much of the upper part of the tree, the root wad was able to overbalance the rest of the log—and the tree had fallen back up.

We fished the axe and saw out of the river (the water bottle had floated off before we could collect ourselves) and carried the rest of the shingle bolts up to the path. Considering the excitement of what had just happened, we were both unusually quiet. Tom was especially subdued. I know how he felt; it has taken me a long time to get used to it, too. It's not an easy feeling—standing there in the woods, knowing that all the trees are laughing at you.

Chapter 2. Tools

He was a left-handed man. Other workmen might be
annoyed by apprentices or ignorant boys using their sharp
axes; but you didn't do that twice with George Cook's axe—it
was too dangerous a trick.
—George Sturt, *The Wheelwright's Shop* (1923)

The beech body of this 150-year-old jack plane still retains the imprint of the hands of its owner.

Like trees and people, tools have a definite life cycle—brashness in youth, mellowness in maturity, and degeneration in extreme old age. When first made, even the best tools possess only potential. The edges are rough, the metal and wooden parts are still unsure of each other. When put to use, however, the tool becomes the link between man and his material. The time served in this situation endows the tool with experience and understanding. The tool comes to know the craftsman's hands, just as they come to know the tool. Contact with the material also has its effect, smoothing and mellowing the initial resistance of the tool to its work.

For a tool to achieve this maturity, it must first possess the potential for such growth. A tool that is so poorly made that it will not last long enough to reach maturity is simply a waste of money and effort. The tool must also have been properly designed with the capacity to do the job for which it is intended.

Second, the craftsman must nurture and encourage a tool. Tools thrive with loving use and perish under thoughtless abuse. Even a tool with great potential can become only as good as the mind that controls it. Neglecting or abusing tools is wasteful and inexcusable.

Finding Tools

I buy almost all of my tools at antique markets, junk dealers, and flea markets, where I look for tools that have seen the care of experienced hands and that have the potential to grow in my own. Some tools were made or have become by use left-handed; I cannot use these, but I pick them up for my occasional southpaw student.

When considering a new tool, I again look for the potential for growth. I ask myself if this tool can ever become a great one. If the answer is in doubt, I save my money. Life is both too long and too short to spend with any but the best.

The Tools

AXES AND ADZES. Axes and adzes are "impact" tools. The long handle allows the user to give velocity to the cutting edge, which then severs the fibers of the wood. The handle, or helve, of a felling axe is usually 32 or so inches long, and the head weighs from three to five pounds. The cutting edge, or bit, is centered in line with the eye for the handle and is beveled on both sides. The common hatchet is just a small version of a felling axe.

The bit of the broad axe and the broad hatchet is beveled on only one side. When its handle is offset to one side, it may be used for cross-grain squaring of horizontal timbers without damage to the hands. Adzes also have variations in size and weight and come in both two-handed, or "foot," adzes and smaller, single-handed models. The weight of a foot adz varies according to the fineness of the work for which it is intended —heavy hewing or light finishing. Adzes for use in hollowing are usually curved in the bit and head. Handles on most adzes are easily

Axes and adzes (clockwise from top): Two large broad axes, felling axe and carpenter's adz, heavy felling axe and small broad axe, two single-beveled hewing hatchets, two double-beveled hatchets, gutter adz, bowl adz, carpenter's hammer-adz, and cooper's adz.

removable to allow for sharpening the single inside bevel on a grindstone.

SPLITTING TOOLS. Iron wedges driven by a sledgehammer are the most common splitting tools. Their functions are combined in the heavy splitting maul. Once a split is begun, it may be continued with wooden gluts driven by a wooden maul. These wooden wedges and hammers are often reinforced by iron rings to minimize splitting.

The froe is an L-shaped splitting tool; holding the froe by its wooden handle, the user drives the blade into the wood with a one-handed maul. Once the froe is driven in, the handle becomes a lever to continue the split down through the wood. The froe is often used with a splitting or riving break made from a forked

tree. This break allows leverage to be selectively applied to one side of the wood or the other to control the direction of the split. The best maul for use with the froe is one made from the taproot of a hickory tree; its natural hardness helps it endure the pounding against the narrow metal blade.

HANDLING TOOLS. The raw material of woodworking can be plenty heavy. Once a tree is down, the real work of moving it begins. Leverage tools like the jack and cant hooks aid in rolling logs about; the bigger the log, the bigger the hook and lever that is needed. By setting two cant hooks or similar devices on opposite sides of a log, two people can lift and carry it. Timber carriers are specifically designed for this job of hauling logs by hand; they usually have a

pivot where the hooks attach to the handle to enable the carriers to negotiate between trees. When two timber carriers are used with four people to carry a log, more weight is carried by the set of hooks that is set furthest from its end of the log. Set both carriers equidistant from the ends for equal loads. Log carts can do the work of ten men. They lift the log, roll it to its destination, and set it down again.

HOLDING TOOLS. With the shaving horse, a foot-operated vise, both hands are left free to work the wood. A quick release of foot pressure permits rapid readjustment of the workpiece. The more conventional screw vise on the workbench is adjustable for various widths of work by moving the peg on the bottom arm. The end vise on the bench can accommodate different lengths of work through the use of "dogs," which fit into sockets set along the length of the bench top. The bench hook not only holds stock as it is sawed or chiseled but protects the bench top from damage during these operations. The holdfast, which fits into a slightly oversized hole, is driven down with its pad on top of the work until it becomes cocked in the hole and holds the piece secure; it can be instantly released by a tap on its backside. A hewing bench serves as a sawhorse and as a chopping block; the cross-grain work surface will not grab the hatchet as the end grain of a stump will. The spike dog is a large iron staple; driven into a log being worked on, it holds the log steady on the cross or support logs.

Splitting tools (clockwise from top): Froe, froe club made from hickory tap root, riving brake made from a forked tree, hickory maul, splitting maul, two dogwood gluts, iron wedge, and iron glut with wooden insert.

Handling tools (clockwise from top): Timber cart, timber carriers, cant hook, jack hook.

SAWS. Saws can be grouped according to the direction of the grain they are intended to cut. Acting like a row of tiny knives, crosscut saws sever the cross grain of the wood. Ripsaws cut along the grain, like a row of tiny chisels. In both kinds of saws, the individual teeth are alternately bent, or set, to opposite sides to create a cut, or kerf, that is wider than the blade of the saw.

Bow or frame saws rely on a wooden body to maintain the tension of the narrow blade. Panel or open hand saws have enough width and stiffness to support themselves. The fine thin blades of dovetail and tenon saws are stiffened by a "back." The blades are generally not braised to the back, but are held by friction. If the blade of a backsaw appears to be warped, it may have just worked loose from the back. It may often be straightened by hitting the top edge of the back down on a flat wooden surface to reset the blade.

DRAWKNIVES AND SHAVES. Drawknives come in varied forms for different jobs. Almost all of them are pulled toward the user with two hands and have a single-beveled cutting edge. Some are designed to be used only with the flat of the blade against the work; others can be used with the bevel of the blade against the work for cutting into concave areas. The blade may also be convex or concave along its length and used in hollowing or rounding surfaces, a common operation in cooperage. Drawknives with heavily bent or circular shapes are called inshaves or scorps.

Although spokeshaves and their cousins share several features with planes, they are used like drawknives, and for similar operations. They have either a wooden or a metal body and can be adjusted to make a coarser or finer cut. The blade, or iron, may be straight, convex, or concave with the underside, or bed, of the body shaped to match. This group of tools includes some odd homemade variations to suit the needs of particular jobs, such as smoothing the interior of hewn wooden bowls.

CHISELS, GOUGES, AND MALLETS. Chisels may be pushed with the hand or driven with a mallet. Paring chisels are for light work. Having a bevel angle as low as 15°, these are primarily intended to be used with hand pressure. Framing, firmer, and mortice chisels are heavier and stronger: they are usually driven with a mallet. Their bevels may be from 20°, to 30°, with the thicker bevel for rougher work. The largest chisel of all, however, the slick or broad chisel, is intended only to be pushed; with its weight it can be used to shape large surfaces.

Gouges also vary according to the roughness of the work for which they are intended. They can also be classed according to whether the bevel is on the inside of the curve (in-cannel) or the outside (out-cannel); the latter is the more common and useful of the two. Socket chisels with iron rings around the striking end of the wooden handle may be struck with a metal hammer, but a wooden mallet will be more satisfactory both for the life of the tool and for ease of working. Wood drives a chisel; metal distorts and then drives it.

PLANES. Although we think of old planes as being all wood with a metal blade, the ancient Romans had metal-bodied ones. In the late nineteenth century many planes were made with wooden bodies and metal adjustment mechanisms. You adjust, or set, the all-wood planes by tapping them with a mallet. To lower the

Holding tools (clockwise from top): Hewing bench, shaving horse, spike dog, holdfast, bench vise, bench hook.

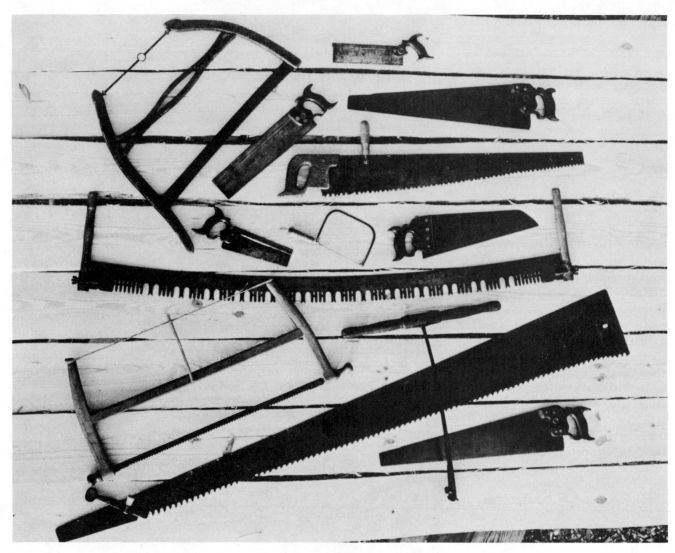

Saws (left to right from top): Bucksaw, dovetail saw, tenon saw, crosscut panel saw, one-man crosscut saw, small tenon saw, coping saw, fine-toothed panel crosscut saw, two-man crosscut saw with perforated lance-toothed pattern, turning saw, two-man rip or "pit" saw with tiller handle dismounted, panel ripsaw.

blade, or iron, as it is properly called, and deepen the cut, you tap on the front end grain of the plane body. By tapping on the back end or on the strike button on top of the nose of the plane you raise the iron and reduce the depth of cut. The wood in front of the iron on the underside, or bed, of a plane pushes down on the surface to be planed and prevents splintering ahead of the cut. As the bed wears down, the opening of the throat grows larger; in time, it may have to be repaired with a patch to keep it sufficiently narrow. However, if the throat is too narrow or rough for the shavings removed by the iron, it will choke; adjustment is

made by opening the throat or reducing the depth of the iron.

Planes also vary according to their purpose. A short plane with a deep-set iron removes a lot of wood quickly and rides down into hollows. A longer plane rides over hollows and removes high spots first to bring a surface perfectly level. The shape of the bed and the iron determines the final shape of the planed surface. A narrow, square iron will make a groove; a wide iron with a gap in the middle will leave a tongue. Molding planes can create every shape imaginable, either by themselves or in combination with other planes. A plane that is intended to work across

Drawknives and shaves (left to right from top): Scorp, bowl shave, cooper's inside drawknife, inshave, wood-bodied spokeshave with cutting iron removed, combination spokeshave with concave and straight irons, drawknife with "dropped" handles, drawknife with straight handles, one iron-bodied and two wooden-bodied spokeshaves.

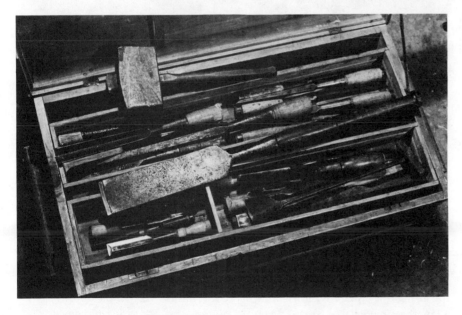

Chisels and gouges (left to right from top): Corner chisel, morticing chisels, slick, bench and paring chisels, gouges.

the grain will often have a diagonal or skewed iron to produce a smooth cut and may also incorporate a down-cutting knife blade, or "snicker," to precede the plane iron and sever the grain for a smooth edge. Various sorts of fences and stops control the depth and width of the cut. To

avoid damaging the iron, always lay a plane down on its side.

MEASURING AND MARKING TOOLS. The human body is the basis for most measurements; you are still furnished with the equipment for measuring inches, cubits, yards, and

feet. Two-foot folding rules and the proverbial "ten-foot pole" will do for greater precision. The steel square is both a rule and right angle and an aid in computing angles for laying out joints and framing rafters. The adjustable bevel can be set to remember any angle. The try square

Planes (clockwise from top): Tongue plane, plow plane, two molding planes, large all-wood jointer plane, wood-and-iron-bodied jack plane, handmade panel-raising plane, dogwood rounder plane (on stick), apple-wood fork-staff plane.

has a wide shoulder to hold against one of the faces of a board to be squared. Scribes are knives or points that make fine, permanent marks. The marking gauge incorporates a scribe and a fence; a gauge that has two or more points can be used to mark several measurements at once. Gauges that scribe with a knife blade are called cutting gauges; they are used for slicing the wood as well as for marking it. Dividers are handy for laying out equal divisions along a length of material. A snap line will mark a long straight line when used with charcoal, chalk, or berry juice.

BORING TOOLS. The cutting end of a boring tool acts like a small rotary chisel. A central lead screw feeds this cutting edge into the work on most regular twist augers. The chisel edge is often preceded by

down-cutting "lips," which sever the cross grain ahead of it to produce a smoother cut. The twist of the body of the auger acts as a chip elevator. The twist auger is a relatively new invention; it became common only after 1800. Before that time, augers had no lead screw, lips, or twist. Large augers are usually provided with a T handle or are designed to be mounted in a device called a boring machine that gives continuous rotary motion to the auger. Another type of auger, the center bit, like smaller twist augers, is designed to be used in a brace. It has a lip and cuts a clean hole, but has only a central pike rather than a lead screw and has no twist to remove chips.

Sharpening

It is a waste of time to try to work with tools that are not properly sharpened, and with axes and adzes it can be dangerous as well. A blunt or rough cutting edge that will not readily sever the fibers of the wood will obviously require more effort to use. The work is already hard enough without having the tools working against you.

However, a keen edge is only one aspect of sharpness. Even though it is honed to surgical fineness, the cutting edge of a tool will not cut well unless it is properly aligned with the body of the tool.

Improper sharpening can be a source of great frustration. If you don't understand how a tool works, you can easily work for hours with

expensive sharpening stones and still end up with a tool that is as good as useless. Only a correctly shaped edge will efficiently transmit the force through to the wood.

A poorly shaped cutting edge on an axe can be a genuine hazard. To chop wood the blade of the axe must enter the wood at an angle and pop out a chip. If the bevels that form the cutting edge are fat and rounded, one of them may contact the surface of the wood before the cutting edge does and cause the axe head to glance off. If, however, the angle formed by the bevels is too narrow, the axe may sink in and stick and grab in the wood. The proper shape and angle of the bevels are quite specific for different jobs, different woods, whether the wood is frozen or not, and individual preference. I sharpen my axe by hooking one leg

Measuring and marking tools (clockwise from upper left): Snap line and reel, try square, plumb bob, scribe or scratch awl, double-pointed morticing gauge, marking gauge, cutting gauge, framing square, dividers, two-foot folding rule, scribing knife, adjustable bevel.

Boring tools (clockwise from top): Boring machine, T-handled spiral auger, large spiral auger, pre-1800 "shell" auger, pump drill, "German" brace with center bit, modern ratchet brace with set of spiral bits.

over the handle to hold the head on my knee so that I can sharpen it with a file. I like to work fast and will often stop and reshape the bevel if the axe doesn't feel as though it's cutting right in a particular tree. I put on a wider angle when cutting frozen wood or if the bit sticks in the cut, and a narrower angle if it isn't sinking in well enough. I also use different felling axes with different-shaped bits and try to take the right one with me when I go to the woods.

Chisel-edged tools, with a bevel on one face and a flat on the other, are quite different from the knife-edged, double-beveled felling axes. For one, their steel is generally harder, and a file will barely cut them. Chisels, adzes, plane irons, and the like, should be ground to shape with abrasive stones, then polished with finer and finer stones until they have a mirror finish. The essential difference, however, is the shape of the edges of these tools. The angle of the edge is formed by the intersection of the bevel and the flat. This angle varies from 15° on fine paring chisels to over 30° on heavy framing chisels and adzes. The integrity of the flat side of a chisel-edged tool must be maintained. The slightest rounding over of this side not only increases (blunts) the angle of the cutting edge but also changes the angle of attack from which the tool must be operated in order for the edge to make contact with the wood. Keep the flat side flat.

I grind my tools to shape on a foot-powered sandstone grinding wheel. It cuts fast, never overheats the tool, and puts on an edge that is fine enough for many jobs. If you are looking to buy an old used sandstone, pass up one that looks as though it has been left standing in water in a trough set beneath it. A sandstone must be kept wet as you use it, but if it is left standing in

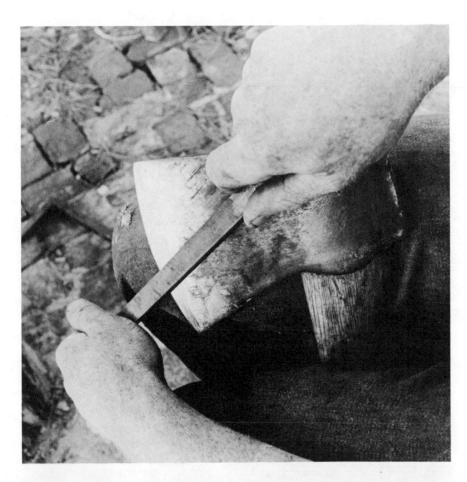

Felling axes sharpen fast with a file.

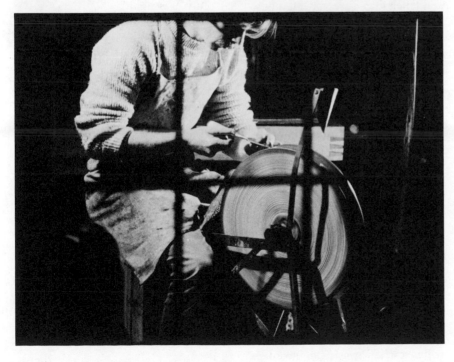

A sandstone grinding wheel works quickly and safely. Hold the tool steady to make the bevel flat rather than rounded.

The feather edge shows as a bright line.

This white clay stone needs only spit to keep it working. Hold the tool steady at a consistent angle to prevent rounding over.

water, it will be softened on that side and quickly wear out of round.

As you grind the bevel of a tool to shape, you will reach a point when the metal on the very edge will be worn so thin that it no longer has the stiffness to press against the stone and will begin to form a fine feather edge. When this happens, it's time to move to a finer stone. I usually remove the feather edge by working it back and forth with my thumb until it all breaks off. The final honing and polishing must be done with very fine stones. I like stones that can be used with water rather than oil and almost exclusively use white clay stones that are made for sharpening straight razors. I have never bought one of these new because they generally run about twenty-five cents at flea markets. They cut quick and hone the edge as sharp as I ever need.

To check the flatness of the flat side, I hold it down flat on top of my left thumbnail and try to shave off a curl. If I have to tilt the tool up to get it to grab, I know that the flat side is rounded over. This side must then be polished flat or the

edge must be ground back on the beveled side until the rounded-off length of the flat is removed.

I met the Deacon years after he had retired. His shop had changed hands and fallen into disrepair. He knew how interested I was in the old ways, and so we would talk for hours about red-heart cypress, bench drills, wheelwrighting, wrought iron, and the like.

I once asked him, as one who should know, which was the best way to turn a wet sandstone grinding wheel, toward or away from you?

"Always away from you," he said.

Now, I had been at this long enough to have formed the opinion that there is seldom one right answer to questions like this. Seeing that he was not going to carry on with any further explanation, I proceeded to expound on the debate as I understood it.

"Well, you know," I said, "I've heard both ways; some want you to go away from you so that the heat will be carried away from the edge of

the tool. Now, I know that the water dripping on the sandstone keeps it from ever getting very hot so that can't really be important. Some say you want to go towards yourself and the tool so that you won't draw out a wire edge and you can get it sharp faster. But you say away from you is right."

"Always go away from you," he repeated.

"But why is that? What are you doing to the edge that makes that better? Do you want to draw out a wire edge? Is that why you do it?"

"No," he said, laughing. "If you turn towards you, you throw water in your lap."

Chapter 3. Gluts and Mauls

The rail splitter, who was ordered not to strike the iron
wedge with an iron axe . . . , could work with . . . a makeshift,
axe-cut, larger wooden wedge, still called . . . the 'glut'.
—Henry Mercer, *Ancient Carpenter's Tools* (1929)

The most basic tools are the wooden club, or maul, and the heavy wooden wedge, or glut. Older than history, they were probably the first refinements of the caveman's unfashioned stick and stone tools. With them you can split stone blocks to build pyramids or split trees to make the rest of the things in this book.

Consider how these tools work. The handle of the maul enables you to accelerate a mass (the head) over a greater distance than you could with, say, a rock in your bare hands. When struck by the maul, the glut, with its wedge shape, converts the force of the forward motion of the maul into pressure exerted to the sides and splits the log.

Of course, it doesn't help get the wood split any faster to think in such analytical terms, but simplicity is a good teacher. Think about what you, the wood, and the tools are doing as you make these simple things.

Finding a Tree

Begin by going into the woods. Now, you may say, "Well, that's it for me. I don't have access to any woods." But if you live in North America, this should not be the case. If you don't know where to begin, contact your state or county forester. Part of their job is getting people and trees together.

One more thing. I'll be speaking about hickory and dogwood, but don't worry if they don't grow in your part of the country. They are chosen for their toughness and density. Dogwood, in particular, is very resistant to splitting. You could also use Osage orange, ash, scrub oak, or simply the hardest, most shock-resistant wood available to you in your area. Use what the people who came before you used.

So shoulder your axe and begin the search. For the maul, you're looking for a small hickory tree that's a good solid 6 inches thick at the base and straight on up for at least a yard or so.

Felling

When you find a tree that looks right, that looks like it has a maul inside it, pause a minute before you start cutting. Acknowledge the presence of the tree and what it has been doing all these years. You are about to kill this tree. Let it know that you appreciate what it has been doing and accept the responsibility of giving it a second life.

While you're looking up re-

spectfully, look carefully among the branches to see if any dead limbs or "fool killers" wait there; knocked loose, one of these can drive you into the ground like a tent peg. Decide which way you want the tree to fall. Usually this is the best clear path for the tree to the ground— meaning, it shouldn't hang up in the other trees on the way down. A tree that has a decided lean to one side is best felled at right angles to that lean to prevent it from falling prematurely and splintering at the base.

Stand to the side of the tree at a right angle to the direction you want the tree to fall. If you are cutting right-handed, you need to be on the left-hand side of the tree as you face it from the direction you want it to fall. Check around and be sure that the axe head won't catch on

Your whole body works when you fell a tree. The right hand starts at the top of the axe helve.

It slides down to meet your left hand by the time the axe is parallel with your body.

anything as you swing it, causing it to hook and sink into your leg.

Control is important here. The idea is to "hinge" the tree down right where you want it. Begin by making a felling cut two-thirds of the way through the trunk on the side that you want the tree to fall to. The unsupported weight of the tree over this open space is going to start the tree in that direction. Then make a second cut on the back side of the tree just above this first one. The wood that is left between the two cuts will lead the tree to fall in the desired direction.

Right-handed axe work starts with the right hand up near the head of the axe. The left hand is kept at the bottom of the handle, or helve. As the bit of the axe is thrown into the cut, the right hand slides down to

meet the left. A good axe handle with plenty of "whip" will give a higher impact velocity and do more work than a stiff one.

The blade or bit of the axe must enter the wood at about a 45° angle to have any effect. Too low an angle and the axe will glance off the work and hurt someone. Coming in at 90° to the work has little effect because there is no place for the wood to go to allow the axe to cut in. Cutting trees is not like slicing carrots. For an axe to penetrate the wood at 90° to its surface it would either need to sever the top from the stump in one blow, as in chopping kindling, or it would have to compress the end grain of the wood above and below the cut. Both of these are, of course, unlikely in a tree worth working with. If, however, the axe comes in

at the proper angle, it will remove a chip of wood that will take with it much of the resistance to the penetration of the axe.

To keep this proper angle available to you as you cut deeper into the tree, start with an opening that is, on the surface, one-half to two-thirds of the diameter of the tree. Keep popping out chunks of wood with alternating top and bottom cuts until you are on the far side of the heart of the tree. Be sure that you have the deepest part of the cut straight and at right angles to the desired direction of fall.

Now change sides and cut in on the back side of the tree, just above where you made the first cut. When you get close to the finish, stop. Check the wind, as it may have changed. See that everyone and

Throw the bit into the tree—don't push it.

When your first cut is over halfway through, make the second cut just above it on the opposite side. The tree should "hinge" down precisely where you want it.

everything is clear in front and in back. Everything OK? Finish the cut, yell "Timber!!" and let it fall.

Bucking the Log

Once the tree is on the ground, chop off the limbs and branches by swinging up on them from below the crotch that they form with the main stem. You may want to leave one of the limbs that points straight up to use for turning the log during the next process, which is cutting the log to length, or "bucking."

Cut the log at the desired point by standing on it and making two V cuts, one from either side, that meet in the middle. Back when firewood was the only fuel, every piece had to be cut this way. Since you want to be able to get it out in as few trips as possible, cut the tree into pieces that are about as long as you can manage to carry out on your shoulder. You can cut these pieces to length once you get them home.

Gluts

While you're out there, cut some 4- to 5-inch-diameter dogwood or other tough stuff to use for making the gluts. When you get back home, make a pair of gluts first. They may

Buck the log to a length that you can carry out of the woods.

Cut in halfway from both sides.

be helpful in making the maul.

Using the bucksaw, cut off a length of the dogwood that is twice as long as you want your gluts to be, about 2 feet or so. You cut the piece long so that you will have something to hold on to as you do your hatchet work. The hatchet for this job is a regular, knife-edged "camp" hatchet. This is just a smaller version of the axe that you used to cut down the tree; the blade is beveled to the cutting edge from both sides. Chop half of the length into a wedge shape. When you finish one end, flip the piece over and chop down the other half. Now crosscut the piece in half with the saw and you have two wedges and still have ten fingers. To finish up, chop off any remaining bark and all of the square corners. Put these green gluts away to dry very slowly in, say, a humid cellar or under the bathroom sink to prevent cracking, or "checking." Dogwood dries to an incredibly tough wood that will not split. That's why you can use it for wedges.

With all this chopping you're going to need something to chop on. A stump of wood about 2 feet tall is good. Even better, though, is a hewing bench made from half a log. With this you chop into cross grain rather than end grain. When the hatchet hits the bench, it won't stick into the cross grain, as it will into the end grain of even an elm stump.

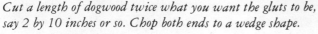

Cut a length of dogwood twice what you want the gluts to be, say 2 by 10 inches or so. Chop both ends to a wedge shape.

Saw the two gluts apart with a bucksaw.

Take off the corners with a hatchet.

The single-beveled hewing hatchet makes quick work of squaring off the end grain on the maul.

Chop in a neck all the way around where you want the head of the maul to be.

Roughing Out the Maul

Now for the maul. Saw or chop off a 38-inch length of the butt end of the hickory log. All that remains is to chop and split away enough of this log to make a handle out of all but 8 inches of its length. This last section, the head, is left full round.

The best tool for these next steps is another sort of hatchet, a broad or hewing hatchet. This hand axe is the main shaping tool of the traditional woodworker. The blade of the hewing hatchet is beveled on one side only, like a chisel. Having one side flat and one side beveled means that the cutting edge will "lead" to the flat side when it enters the wood. The flat on my right-handed hewing hatchet is on the left as I hold it, the bevel on the right. This causes the cut to lead to the left.

The utility of this arrangement is best seen in practice. Start by squaring off the butt end of the hickory where the felling axe did

its work. Set the log on the bench with the butt end to the right and hold it down with your left hand. Cut straight down with the hewing hatchet, dead on the line where you want the end flattened off. When you have a lot of waste to remove, alternate these straight-down blows with angled cuts coming in from the right. With practice, you will find that you can square off end grain smooth and flat.

Now move down 8 inches and circle the log with angled cuts coming in from the right. The bevel of the hatchet is down, or against, the work. Go all the way around, then turn the log end for end and again circle it with angled blows, still coming in from the right. Each time you hit, a chunk of wood should pop out. Keep this up, going all the way around and turning the maul end for end, until you have cut down to a 2-inch diameter, dead in the heart of the log.

This could be done with a saw, but the hatchet is the right tool for

two reasons. First, the saw can make only a straight cut, and the junction of the handle and the head should be a gentle rather than a sharp change of cross section. This keeps stresses from concentrating at a single point and helps prevent breakage. Second, you can do it twice as fast with a hand axe. Better and faster—reasons enough.

Now that you have cut in the neck all the way around, you can begin splitting away the bulk of the wood to form the handle. Start at the far end and drive in an iron wedge just to one side of what you want to leave for the handle. Watch the grain carefully to see that your split won't run down into the head. Any sort of wedge will do. You can start the split with your felling axe and finish up with your gluts (even if they're not dry yet), or you can do it all with regular iron splitting wedges. The tool that is just right for this job, however, is a dull but powerful fellow called the froe. Also known as a fromard, a board axe, and a dozen other names, it consists of a heavy blade about a foot long with an eye for the handle at one end. The L-shaped froe is used with a one-handled maul or froe club, which drives the blade into the work. The handle of the froe provides the leverage to continue the split down through the work. You can still find froes at junk dealers or make one yourself. So, using a froe or wedges, split away the extra wood, then chop off any thick spots down to about a 2-inch diameter with the hand axe.

Using the Drawknife

Smoothing down this rough-split surface is done with a drawknife. Unlike froes, drawknives are still to be found in hardware stores. They come in many different styles and sizes, but basically they are all single-beveled blades with a handle on each end. As its name and the position of the handles indicate, the drawknife is pulled toward the user with both hands.

Because the cutting edge of the drawknife is single beveled, it can be used two ways: with the bevel down, against the work, or with the bevel up, with the flat against the work. Bevel down is the only way to work effectively on concave surfaces, but that's not the only time you would want to use it that way. On straight surfaces, you can often control the depth of the cut better by having the bevel to rock against the work to raise or lower the leading edge. In other words, you can steer the cut

Drive in the froe from the bottom.

Split away the excess wood. Here, the handle of the froe club holds the split open as the froe is worked downward.

A Root Maul

Most wooden mallets are used only to pound wood. An exception to this is the club or maul used to drive the iron froe. Ordinary wooden mauls cannot long endure constant pounding on metal. Here is a situation where you want to dig your wood up rather than cutting it down. Root wood grows from the inside out and is further toughened by the knots of the feeder roots. Dig out a small hickory or dogwood tree, chop it to shape with the head beginning at what was ground level, and you'll wear out twelve pairs of shoes before you wear out your maul.

Digging a root maul. Hickories like this run deep; you'll need a sharp mattock. Dogwoods are shallow rooted and easier to cut free. This is why they tend to die in droughts; their roots don't go deep enough.

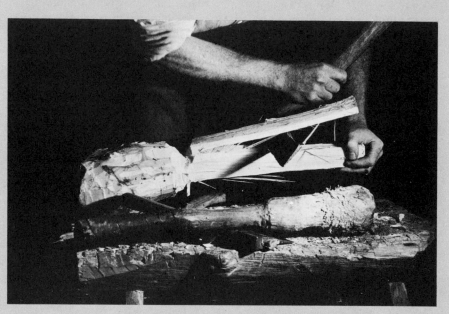

The froe club in the foreground hasn't had a vacation in six years and has quite a few more to go.

better. Holding the flat against the work gives straighter cuts on straight-grained wood. The flat tends to keep the blade on an even keel.

Every drawknife has its own personality. Much of this personality is influenced by the angle of the handles relative to the flat of the blade. If the handles are in line with the flat, the drawknife can be used with the bevel up or down with equal ease. But when the handles drop down on the flat side, the drawknife is strictly for bevel-up, flat-down use. The drop of the handles counteracts the tendency of the flat to dig into the wood, but makes it very hard to use the tool with the bevel down.

The job now is to smooth off the roughed-out maul handle. Since both of your hands will be occupied in using the drawknife, you'll need to brace the maul against your body as you work on it. The shaving horse described in the following chapter is made specifically for holding draw-knife work like this, but you'll be using the maul and gluts to make the shaving horse. First things first.

Finishing Up with the Spokeshave

Carefully applied, the drawknife can give a very smooth surface, but one last tool could be used here to finish the job. The spokeshave is another

Shave it with a drawknife.

Finish up with a spokeshave.

two-handled bladed device. Set in a wood or iron stock with straight handles out to the sides, the blade protrudes from the bottom, or bed, of the stock and can be adjusted for a specific depth of cut, just like a carpenter's plane. A finely set spokeshave will allow you to refine a shape with less trouble than you can with a drawknife. Spokeshaves are still made in a variety of forms; some combine a concave and a straight blade, side by side on the same tool. They are easy to find in just about any hardware store.

So far you have been chopping and splitting away in green wood. This is what you want to be doing. The wood responds best to these shaping tools when it is still green and soft. But now, with the spokeshave, you may find the wood tearing up and jamming in the mouth of the shave. Many woods, hickory in particular, need to be drier in order to work well with the finer tools. If the spokeshave doesn't seem to work right, let the wood dry out a bit and try again.

Let the gluts and the maul dry slowly in a cool and shady spot to become tough enough to withstand hard use. Except for construction timbers, this is the last time that we will be using whole stems in the full round. The uneven shrinkage of the grain in whole tree sections causes such checking problems that they should be used only in the roughest work or in wood with thoroughly interlocked grain. Even after months or years of drying, a glut or maul can split wide open after being brought into a dry, heated house. Always keep them outside. The dogwood and the hickory butts should be tough enough to hang together during the stresses of drying if you give them sufficient time to make the adjustment.

Think about what you have done so far. You found a tree that had the right species and individual characteristics. You felled it and while it was still green and soft, you shaped it by chopping and splitting. For the final finishing work you waited

for the wood to dry and become more workable with finer tools. You matched the tools not only to the scale of the task but to the changing nature of the material itself. With the addition of the special needs of joining two pieces of wood together, these are the basic skills of woodworking.

Chapter 4. Shaving Horses

Tom sat on a shingle-horse in the open door of the mill.
A warm May breeze blew lightly through the open window,
and the afternoon sunshine floated in upon the floor.
—Mabel O'Donnell, *Singing Wheels* (1954)

Working at the shaving horse is about the most satisfying work a person can do. You sit down, put a rough-split billet of wood in the jaws of the horse, and clamp it tight with your foot on the bottom of the lever. The horse, which you have tailored to fit your body, holds the work-piece perfectly positioned as you sail through it with a razor-sharp draw-knife. To change the position of the piece, you just let off a little with your foot, turn the work the way you want it, put the foot pressure back on, and keep on shaving. It's a very fast way to work wood; you're up to your seat in shavings in no time. Using a shaving horse, you can turn a tree into axe handles, rakes, grain shovels, or chairs in an afternoon.

Shaving horses have different names in different regions and differ-ent designs for different trades. Old chair makers in my county usually refer to them as "drawbreaks." The German name for them is *Schnitzel-bank*. These regional variations in design and nomenclature are im-portant to us all. Your part of the forest has its own peculiar heritage. You may be the only one who can preserve it before it is totally forgotten. Find out how they did it where you live; then at least someone will remember.

The shaving horse shown in this chapter is the central tool in both of my occupations, teaching and pro-duction for sale. I am going to show you how to make a shaving horse from a single 6-foot-long log. You use the weaknesses of the wood to help you split out the plank for the bench, the four legs, and the vise parts; then you use the strengths of the wood to rejoin these pieces into your horse.

The Right Wood

Red oak and white oak are the woods that I use most often for shaving horses. Oak is plenty strong; yet it's easy to work with. Among the hundred or so horses that I have done with my students, I have seen them made from red cedar, maple, pine, and walnut. Most of the transformation from tree to horse is accomplished by splitting, so elm or gum would not be a good choice. Choose a tree of a suitable species that shows in its bark that it will split relatively straight. Look for a section about 6 feet long and from 10 to 12 inches thick where the bark runs straight up and down without excessive spiraling. Small knots are alright, but heavy corkscrewing and large limbs should say "firewood" to you.

After cutting the log, you should first split it in half. If you have cut the tree down out in the woods by yourself, splitting a log this size in half will be the only way you'll be able to carry it out. Even then, it's about as much as one strong person can carry. So take your wedge with you to the woods, along with a clear idea of what you're going to be making.

Splitting Out the Bench

Use an iron wedge to start the crack in the end grain. You need to drive this wedge in just enough to score a straight crack all the way across. Once you have started the split, use gluts to finish it up, leapfrogging them until you have the log in two. Don't worry about a moderate spiral or the roughness of this first split. It all works out in the end.

Choose the better of the two halves to make the main plank of the

This 10-inch-diameter, 6-foot length of red oak will make one shaving horse. Start by splitting it in half.

bench. You are going to have to split off enough of the round, bark side to leave a plank that's about 3 inches thick. Score across the end grain about 3 inches away from the flat side with the iron wedge. Be sure not to drive it in too far at any point or you can cause a split in the wrong direction. The secret here is to employ a slow, even lift. Use as many gluts and wedges as you can muster and work carefully. Keep tapping in all of the wedges with one hit on each of them, just like playing scales on a xylophone. As you move the wedges down to the far end of the log, the pressure will build up until in one great "pop" the plank jumps free.

Split the plank from the better of the two halves.

An even lift is the key to success.

The Foot Adz

The surface of the plank that you just exposed, the side away from the heart, will be much smoother than the heart side, where all the knots from the youth of the tree have congregated. This smoother side will be the upper surface of the bench. Still, you'll find rough spots, and you may have more twist than you want in the final bench. You can smooth and straighten out the plank in a number of ways, but there is a tool that's made just for this sort of work, the foot adz.

The foot adz is a single-beveled blade mounted on a handle like an axe. However, the blade of the adz is at right angles to the handle with the bevel on the upper side. To use the adz, stand over the work, hold the end of the handle so that it pivots in your left hand, and use your right hand to swing the blade down to take off a chip of wood.

It's not hard to hurt yourself with an adz. The most common accident happens when you are standing over the work with your feet spread on either side to keep your legs clear of a misdirected blow. The edge of the adz will sometimes pick up a chip and hold it so that when you swing down again the adz bounces off and goes into your ankle anyway.

When I work, I usually stand right on the place that I want to adz down. The adz removes a chip directly below the sole of my shoe. To use this method, you need good aim, but it's safer in the long run. It gives you a smoother finish as well because your foot keeps the chip in

Smooth the split-out plank with an adz.

place as it is cut. This keeps the wood from tearing out ahead of the cutting edge and making more rough spots to clean up.

Smooth the plank up a bit, but don't hurt yourself. The only wooden legs you want to have to make are the ones for your shaving horse.

The Legs

Take the bark-side slab that you just split off and saw it into the lengths that you want the legs to be, about 20 inches. Split these lengths into four 2-by-2-inch pieces. These are the rough-split legs, and they can be left rough until they are all driven into their holes in the bench. Once driven in, they can be easily worked smooth with the drawknife.

The legs are driven into holes bored through the plank with a 1 1/4-inch or larger auger. For the legs to be strong enough, they shouldn't be any smaller than 1 1/4 inches. This may cause you some delay as you locate an auger this size, but fortunately, they are not terribly hard to find in junk stores where the rest of these tools come from. The largest regular brace-and-bit-type augers are only 1 inch, so anything over this size will have a T handle on it, and that's just what you want.

To keep the bench from tipping over and to assist the legs in their task of supporting your shifting weight when you work on it, the legs need to splay out evenly to the ends and sides of the bench. This is not as hard as it sounds. Simply bore the hole for one leg and set it in place before you go on to bore the next. When you bore the following hole, lean the auger over so that it matches the angle of the leg that is already in place.

Set the plank on the ground with the top surface down. If the plank still has a bit of twist in it (and mine always do) wedge beneath the two high corners until it sits approximately level. Set the auger on one corner of the plank, about 4 to 6 inches from the end and about 2 inches from the side. Lean the auger out to the corner at an angle of about 35°. Get a good mental image of what's going on and then bore on through.

Hold one of the rough legs beside the hole that you just bored. Then, using the hand axe, chop its end down to a size and an oval shape that can be driven into the hole without splitting the plank. Before you drive the leg into the hole, align the oval shape so that the pressure of the fit will be exerted along the grain of the plank, with the strength of the wood, rather than across the grain, with the weakness of the wood. This helps keep the plank from splitting.

It's safer and smoother to adz directly under the sole of your shoe.

Split out the four legs from the slab removed to make the plank.

Drive in one leg at the appropriate angle and use it as a guide in boring the hole for the next one.

The wood for the legs is green and wet and will, of course, shrink up in a short while. Since the plank is green as well, it will also shrink up around the hole to compensate for this to some extent, but never quite enough. You should leave a longish taper to the legs where they fit into the holes so that, if necessary, you can drive them up tighter as they dry.

With one leg in, you can now bore the next hole, using this first leg as your guide. Tilt the auger away from the first leg until it appears that you have matched its angle and bore away. If you find that the angle of one of the holes is not quite right, you can fix it by cutting a correction angle on the leg where it fits into the hole—a dog leg, if you please.

Turn the bench up on its four legs and see how it stands. Knock legs in further and saw off ends until it sits good and level. The protruding ends of the legs on the top side of the bench can be chopped or sawed off. Wedging the top of the legs is usually unnecessary, but if you need to do it when the bench dries out, be sure to place the wedge so that it exerts pressure along rather than across the grain of the plank. The wedge must be of seasoned wood or it will just bend over when you try to drive it. Use a chisel to start the gap for the wedge.

The Working Parts

So, there's the bench—that's half the battle! Now for the working parts. You still need to make the jaw and arm, or "dumbhead," the ramp, or "riser," that the workpiece sits on, the short block that supports the riser, and, finally, the foot treadle. Make the riser first. Turn to the other half of the log and cut off a

If you wedge the legs from the top, be sure to orient the wedge as shown so that the pressure is exerted along rather than across the grain of the bench top.

This is the easiest way to get the legs evenly splayed.

30-inch length with the bucksaw.

Working very carefully with the froe and wedges, split off a 2-inch-thick slab just as you did the bench plank. This piece may have a twist in it like that of the plank. If you place this piece on the bench with what was the bark side facing down, its twist should cancel out the twist of the bench and be perfectly level at the working end. Sit on the bench with the riser in front of you where it will go. Move the riser up and down so that when you are seated comfortably the riser points right below your elbows. This will be the most effective angle for the workpiece to be held at. Cut a piece of the slab, or what have you, to hold the riser at this height. Chop a seat for this block under the front edge of the riser and then level off the tail end of the riser to get it ready for its final positioning. Don't peg anything together yet; peg only after everything is ready. Always leave your options for correction open as long as possible.

Split the riser from the other half of the tree and chop seats on the side that faced the bark.

In the completed shaving horse any twist in the bench will be canceled out by the reciprocal twist in the riser.

To make the dumbhead, cut the rest of the half log to 36 inches long, which should be more than you will need. It's better to cut it too long than too short. Lay out the dimensions of the head and the arm on the flat face of the log, the head being the upper 6 inches, the arm being the 2-inch-wide extension down the heart of the log. Use a framing square and recheck your measurements to ensure accuracy. Make the cut across the front of the jaw first. Cut in about 2 inches with the bucksaw and then swing around and cut in on the two sides. Turn the piece upside down and begin splitting the waste off the sides. Be careful to watch the run of the grain to ensure that the split will not run inside your saw cuts, break the head, and ruin the piece.

Once you have split the dumbhead down to its rough shape, cut away the throat beneath the jaw and the back side away from where your feet will push. You want to have the arm come forward to meet your feet. The final dimensions of the arm should be 2 inches by 3 inches.

When the arm is completed, turn the piece upside down and chop a sloping face on the dumbhead in whatever style suits you. The shape of the head varies widely from region to region: it's either cut away on the side facing your hands or cut away on the opposing side. I prefer to cut away the side toward my hands, as this gives me clearance to swing them about as I work the drawknife.

Morticing the Bench

The major parts of the shaving horse are now completed. The next step is to lay out and cut the slots in the bench and riser for the arm to move

Make the dumbhead from the remainder of the log by cutting square across the face to a depth of 2 inches to define the gripping surface. Then saw in on both sides, leaving a 2-inch-thick neck in the center.

Split the extra wood off the sides.

in. Set the horse down on its side with the riser and block held in place somehow. Place the dumbhead on the side of the fallen horse in the fully closed position, as though it were gripping nothing. Then, swing the head to its most open position, pivoting around the point where the arm and the riser intersect. Move everything around until you are satisfied that you have located the best pivot point for your dumbhead. Make sure that when the jaws are fully closed, the bottom of the arm doesn't hit the legs. Then, swing the arm back and forth and mark the front and back limits of its travel on the side of the riser and bench. Now, set the horse back on its feet. The marks that you just made give you the end points of the holes, or through mortices, for the travel of the arm; transfer them to their positions in the middle of the bench and riser with a framing square or just by eye. The width of these slots must be laid out as well. You need to be close on the sides of the arm with these mortices, say 2 1/4 inches for a 2-inch-wide arm.

If you have a 2 1/4-inch T-handle auger for the full width of the mortices, so much the better. If not, bore several smaller holes at both ends of where the mortices are to go. Don't bother to bore out the middle sections of these mortices, as they can be removed in short order by chopping out with the hand axe, the same technique used for roughing out dough bowls later on. Clean up the mortices with a chisel and put the arm of the dumbhead through them to see how it fits.

To find the locations for the slots for the dumbhead to move in, set the bench down on its side with the riser and its supporting block held in position. Lay the dumbhead on it so that it appears to be fully closed. Mark the most forward extent of its travel on the riser and the most backward extent on the main bench.

Shape up the dumbhead with the hand axe.

Swing the dumbhead to its fully open position, pivoting it around the intersection with the riser, and mark the limits of its travel.

Set the bench back up on its feet and transfer these marks from the side to the middle of the bench and riser. Bore through the ends of where these slots will be cut.

Remove the wood between the two holes by chopping it out with the hand axe.

Blind Pegging

Blind pegging means that you must bore two holes in two pieces and have them line up perfectly when they are assembled. Start by driving a brad into one of the two pieces and then nipping it off so that only about 1/4 inch protrudes.

Push the two pieces together in the position you want them to be in the final assembly.

Separate them and pull out the brad. It will have left a mark in both pieces. Use these marks to center the auger and bore the peg hole into both pieces. Drive in the peg, cut it to length, and put the two pieces together.

Assembly

Reassemble everything so that the top and bottom are aligned properly and the arm moves freely in the slots. The front block that supports the riser needs to be pegged, top and bottom, to keep it and the riser in place. The underside, where it sits on the bench, must be "blind pegged." To do this, take the block out and in the center of the place on the bench where you want the block to sit drive in a small brad so that it sticks up about 1/4 inch and clip off its head with a pair of nippers. Set the block back into position and press it down

so that the brad leaves a mark in its bottom. Pull the block back out and remove the brad. The mark in the block and the place where the brad was in the bench give you the two points to bore 1/2-inch holes for the peg. The hole for the top peg goes through the top of the riser and can be bored from the top. The pegs need to be dry and oval and set in with the same side-grain clearance used on the legs to prevent splitting.

The back end of the riser where it meets the bench also needs to be pegged securely, as this is always being pulled open when the bench is in use. Two pegs set in at divergent angles work well, but at this point,

when the wood is still green, it is best to put in only one. The reason for this is that the riser shrinks up much faster than the thicker bench plank. Two pegs held apart in the slow-drying, thick bench will cause the faster-shrinking riser to split right up the middle. So wait at least a couple of months or so for both the bench and the riser to season some before setting in the second peg. You can still use the horse with just one peg in the back of the riser. Just take it easy.

You now need to bore the pivot hole. Turn the horse once more on its side and set the dumbhead in its most fully closed position. Use a 3/4

The top peg, which holds the riser on the support block, can be bored through both pieces from the top.

Angled pegs hold the back end of the riser to the bench.

Set the pivot hole by holding the dumbhead in its closed position and boring through the riser.

A foot treadle with a square mortice through it can be set to any height on the dumbhead arm. A small peg keeps it from falling off.

inch or so auger and bore through the riser and the center of the dumbhead arm, clear on through to the other side. The pivot peg you put through here must be dry and a good fit, but loose enough to be easily removed. You may well want to bore a second hole through the dumbhead arm about 3 inches below the first to use when you're working on very big

pieces. Once the pivot peg is in place, you can cut any excess off of the bottom of the arm.

The last step is to put on the foot pad or treadle. You can make this a simple 1 1/4-inch peg set through a hole bored through the bottom of the dumbhead arm, but a better arrangement uses a rectangular piece morticed out so that it will slide up

and down on the arm to adjust for different sized people.

So there you have it. You have turned a tree into a simple machine that will surprise you with the ease and speed with which it allows you to work wood. Your shaving horse will reopen an old dimension in woodworking.

Chapter 5. Rakes

Have a care that the Rake and the Forke lye upright in
thine hand; for if the one end of thy Rake or the side of thy
Forke hang downward then they be neither handsome nor
easie to work with.
—Sir Anthony Fitzherbert, *Booke of Husbandrie* (ca. 1500)

Like any properly made tool, a handmade rake possesses a vitality that makes it a joy to use. The long handle, or stail, perfectly balances the weight of the head. Hickory bows brace the head and help to absorb some of the "thousand natural shocks" that rakes are heir to.

Unlike a romantic hero, a tool gains nothing from a tragically short life. A mindfully crafted wooden rake will endure decades of constant use, long outlasting its machine-made brother. The durability of this tool comes from allowing the natural strength of the tree to pass unbroken into the finished product. Again, this is accomplished by riving out its parts from the log to preserve the flow of the grain, which would be ignored by the ripsaw.

The rake is a tool of many parts. The strength of the individual pieces is of little consequence if the joints between them are not equally strong. Here, and again later on in chair-making, the shrinkage of green wood as it dries can be put to work in making the joints tight and permanent.

Shrinking Wood Together

A circle painted on the side of an inflated baloon will get smaller in diameter as the air is let out. So too will a hole bored in a piece of green wood get smaller as the water in the wood evaporates. If you drive a dry piece of wood into this hole, for example, a dry rake tine into an incompletely seasoned rake head, the unseasoned wood will shrink up around the dry wood and never let it work loose. When making a rake, then, make the tines first and the head last so that only the head still has some shrinking to do upon final assembly.

Tine Making

To make the tines, you need a block of strong, straight-grained wood. I have worked with oak, hickory, ash, sassafras, Osage orange, locust, and willow. Any of these will work, but hickory is probably the best. As always, you must work with what you have. So, fear not. Experiment— something out there will work.

When you find the right wood (it should still be somewhat green), cut it into a block that is as long as you

want the tines to be, about 6 inches or so. Tie the block up around the sides with a stout piece of string or rawhide. This string will hold the block together as you split it into the individual billets. Now, starting in the center of the block, split it in half with a maul and either a froe or a dull hatchet. A small froe made from an automobile leaf spring is ideal for this job. Continue to split the block into 1/2-inch-wide sections parallel to the first split. Again starting in the center, split the block with a series of spaced cuts at right angles to

Split the tines from a block of hickory. This froe is made from an automobile leaf spring.

the first set. The result of this cross hatching is a bundle of perfect 1/2-inch-square billets, all neatly bound with string.

Making these square billets into round tines is the next task. There are at least two ways of doing this.

Square Pegs through Round Holes

The first method is to drive the billets through a sharpened tube called a tine cutter. Mine is made from a sawed-off section of a steel pup-tent pole. The sharpened top end is the part that had been shrunk down to enable the two halves of the tent pole to fit together. The clearance below the narrow neck of the cutting edge is important: a straight piece of pipe will be too tight a fit. If you cannot locate a piece of pipe with a narrowed end, you can either find a pipe the right size and rebore clearance from the bottom or find an oversized pipe and shrink down the top end with hammer and heat. However you do it, the cutting end should have an inside diameter of about 1/2 inch.

To mount the tine cutter on the back end of the shaving horse, first bore one hole to set the cutter in, partway through the bench, then bore a second hole, just the next size smaller, inside the first. This second hole should go all the way through the bench to allow the tines to pass through as they are cut.

Cutting the tines is pleasant work that never fails to fascinate visitors to the shop. You sit backward on the shaving horse and drive the still-green billets through the cutter with a wooden mallet. Grasp each one firmly with the free hand to guide it straight down the tube. Each tine remains in the cutter to be knocked

The tine cutter is narrower at the top to allow the tines to pass through easily.

free by the one following it. The real joy in this work comes from the sound of the tines shooting into the tin bucket placed below the horse. As the bucket fills, the loud "plunk" turns to the mellower tones of the resonant hardwood rods.

Two things to remember with tine cutters. First, don't, even with the wooden mallet, strike the cutting edge when you drive the tines. That would be hard on both the cutter and the mallet. Leave the last bit protruding to be driven on by the next billet. Second, should one of the billets shear off at an angle inside the cutter, clear it out before driving the next one through. Otherwise, you run the risk of immovably wedging the two against each other inside the cutter.

Another Method

Another way to cut the tines involves a simpler tool, often called a dowel-sizing plate. A sizing plate is easy to make, and it will also be needed later to make the bows. All you need is a steel plate about 5/16 inch thick and about as wide and as long as your hand. Drill a hole through the plate the size that you want the tine to be. Then undercut this hole with a drill the next size larger, stopping just short of the other side.

To make tines with the sizing plate, set it on a firm support with the undercut side of the hole facing down and use a heavy hammer to drive the billets on through. Again, do not strike the plate with the last lick or you may well damage the cutting edge.

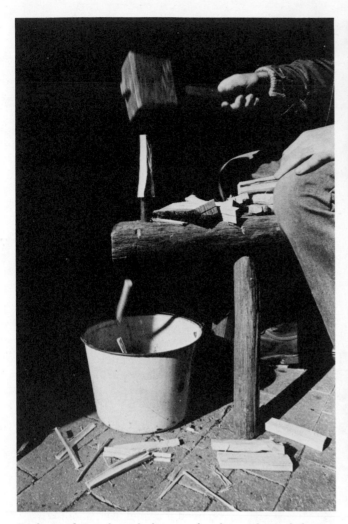

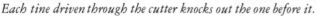

Each tine driven through the cutter knocks out the one before it.   *A sizing plate works just as well as a tine cutter and is easier to make.*

Oval Tines

If you'll remember, the legs for the shaving horse were made oval where they were fitted into the bench in order to get a tight fit without splitting the bench along the grain. This can also be a problem in rake making. All those tines driven into the rake head can easily split it in half if you're not careful. To minimize this danger you can make your tines oval by driving them through an oval hole. It's very simple. Take a rat-tail file and enlarge

the hole in the plate to the desired shape. Or if you're using a tube to cut your tines, hammer it slightly oval.

All of this requires careful judgment. If the billet being cut is too green, it will shrink up too small when dry. On the other hand, the rough billet must be somewhat green in order to be driven easily through the plate or cutter. You can ensure consistent results by using two holes in the plate. Use a 1/2-inch hole for the initial rounding of the billets. Then they can be driven through a final, oval hole, even after they have

thoroughly dried out. The size of this final hole should be gauged from the auger bit that you will use to bore the holes in the head—just a bit bigger than 7/16 inch. The best way to judge the moisture content of the billets, or any piece of wood, is to hold one to your lips. The colder it feels, the wetter it is. Calibrate your senses.

Once you have finished cutting the tines, bundle them up and put them away to dry. You will need an odd number for each rake, usually thirteen or fifteen, but you might as well make more than you need, so you'll have some ready for additional rakes and the countless other needs that they meet about the shop.

Bow Making

The bows hold the rake steady from side to side and act as shock absorbers. As they are only 1/4 inch in diameter and must be able to take hard use, the grain of the wood must run unbroken along their entire length. Make the bows from hickory, ash, fine white oak, or your local favorite. Look in the woods for the same sort of tree that you would want for axe handles; it should be about 6 to 8 inches in diameter with smooth, clear, vertically striated bark. The bark tells you what is going on inside the tree. Clear bark means clear wood.

Fell the tree, cut a 4-foot length, and start splitting. First, split the tree exactly in half, then quarter it, and so on, until you have a pie-shaped section in which the bark face is about two-thirds the width of one of the radial faces. At this point you can start splitting tangentially—meaning, with the growth rings. On these smaller pieces you should soon be able to start the split with the froe and continue it by pulling the two sides apart with your hands. Should the split start to run out to one side, bend the thicker side more sharply as you pull. This will cause the split to run back to the center. Work the pieces down until they are about 3/8 inch square. They can be somewhat rough, but at no point should they be less than 1/4 inch thick. You can now shave them to a rough round with a drawknife.

Split the wood for the bows from straight-grained hickory or ash.

Drawing the Bows

The next step is similar to the rounding of the tines with the sizing plate, but here the pieces are pulled, rather than pounded, through. The plate for this job is made in the same manner as the one used for cutting the tines; in fact, it might as well be the same piece of steel. I use a series of seven holes, from 11/32 inch down to the final 1/4 inch in 1/64-inch steps. These undercut holes can be easily made for you at any machine shop if you don't have suitable drill bits.

Choosing a place where you will have room to work on both sides, mount the plate in a vise or clamp it securely to a beam. The starting end of each piece must first be shaved down so that it will fit through the last and smallest of the holes. With the undercut side of the plate facing you, feed this tapered end into the largest of the holes on the side away from you. Grasp this protruding end with pliers or tongs and pull it through with one long stroke. This first hole is the hardest to pull through, as it is removing the most wood. The work becomes easier as the rod is pulled through successively smaller holes. The last pull will give you a perfect, straight-grained bow rod.

Fresh Stails

The stail is simply a long, straight stick. The obvious way to make one is to seek out a long, straight sapling and try to smooth it up. But it is difficult to shave a sapling smooth with a drawknife; the grain tears out every time the knife encounters one of the tiny knots that dot its length. The grain goes up to the knot on one

Pull the rods through the plate with the undercut side facing you.

The front side of the plate cuts the bow rods like a scraper.

The undercut makes it easier to pull through.

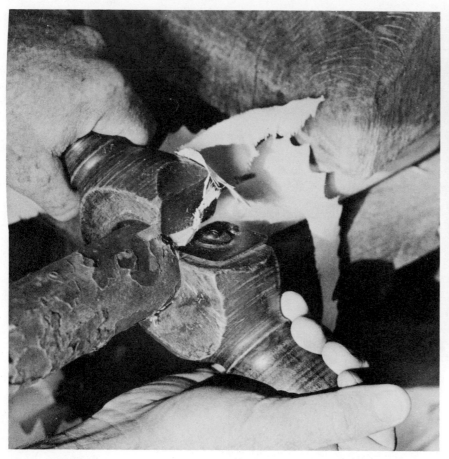

Split out the handles from straight-grained stock.

This stail engine, or rounder plane, works like an endless pencil sharpener to shave this sapling.

side and down away from it on the other side. What is needed is a tool that meets the knots at right angles to the grain.

There is a tool that fits this description, and it is called by many names: nug, witchet, rounder plane, stail engine, and so on. The stail engine, as I'll call it here, is essentially an endless pencil sharpener. It consists of a block of wood with a tapered hole through it. A cutting blade, easily made from a short piece of an old crosscut saw blade, completes the tool. Holding the sapling in a shaving horse or similar contrivance, start the stail engine on one end. "Hand round" the engine down the entire length of the pole,

unwrapping it in one continuous shaving.

Better Stails

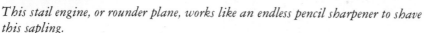

Proper saplings are often not easy to find, and peeling with a stail engine can be tiresome. There is another way to make stails that I find easier and faster and that gives a better product. Again, you need to seek out that proverbial straight-grained, easily split tree. I generally use red or white oak and rive out 6-foot lengths to roughly the proper size. One 10-inch tree will make sixteen stail blanks for each 6-foot

length. These rough splits may then be shaved down at the shaving horse with a drawknife; the clear grain of the mature wood makes this a simple task.

The stails can be made as long as 7 feet and should be just over 1 inch in diameter. They must be quite smooth, as they are constantly sliding through the hands when the rake is in use. The final smoothing can be done with a spokeshave, preferably one with a concave iron, but the best tool for this job is a special plane generally known as a fork-staff plane. Since the blade is set in a long concave bed, this plane removes the high places first, straightening the stail as it rounds and smooths it.

These eight stail blanks are from half of a log. The four hearts on the right are too knotty to use.

Smooth the rough-split stail with the drawknife.

Split-Stail Rakes and Wedged Tines

When the husband sitteth by the fire and hath nothing to doe, then may he make them readie, and toothe the Rakes with dry wilhie wood, and bore the holes with his wimble both above and under, and drive the teeth upward fast and hard, and then wedge them above with dry wood of oake, for that is hard, and will drive and never come out.
—*Booke of Husbandrie*, attributed to Sir Anthony Fitzherbert (1470–1538)

Two alternative styles of stails. The rake in the foreground has wedged teeth.

The Head

Last to be made is the head of the rake. Here again, straight-grained stock should be used. I generally use chestnut, sassafras, or ash. Once you have riven it out to the rough size, trim it with a hand axe and then plane it to the final dimensions. The heads for my thirteen-tine rakes are 25 inches long and 1 inch thick, and taper down from 1 1/2 inches tall at the center to 1 inch at either end.

Lay out the locations for the tine holes by running a marking gauge twice down the underside of the head, gauging first from one side and then from the other. These two lines will give you a constant center even if the head is a bit rough. Using a pair of dividers, find the middle of the length of the head. The center tine will go through here and lock the

This hollow-bottomed fork-staff plane gives the best finish of all.

head to the stail. Starting from this center point, use trial and error to set and reset the dividers to walk off the locations for the remaining tines. For a thirteen-tine rake you must make six moves on either side of the center. When the dividers have been adjusted so that the last hole would be about 7/8 inch from the ends, walk off the lengths again, this time leaving permanent marks to show where to bore the holes. It sounds complicated, but you will find that it works much faster than measuring with a ruler.

Setting the Tines

The holes for the tines must be consistently straight up and down so

Split out the head for the lightest weight and greatest strength.

Plane the head to its final size.

Scribe down the bottom of the head twice with the marking gauge, running the fence against one side and then the other, to find the centerline for the tines.

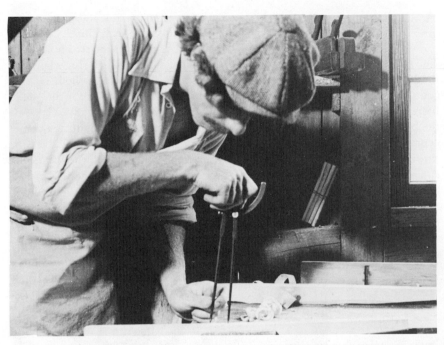

Walk off the locations for the tines with a pair of dividers.

that the tines will be even. Any error in boring the holes will cause gaps between the tines or cause some to lead or follow the rest of the row. To bore the holes correctly, set each tine in place as its hole is bored, then use that tine to guide the auger for the next hole.

Clamp the head, bottom up, firmly in the vise and, using a try square to guide the auger, bore one of the holes on either side of the center hole. Remember, the center hole is bored last. Take one of the seasoned tines and align it so that the oval shape will press along the length of the grain of the head when it is driven in. Use a bit of glue in the hole if you're not absolutely sure of the fit, and drive the tine in until it just clears the other side. Using this tine as a guide, bore the next hole

Get the first tine in straight; then use it to guide all the rest.

Saw all the tines off even.

Point them all with a hand axe.

and drive in its tine. Continue the process until all but the center tine are in place.

Find the shortest tine in the head and cut all the rest to this length so that they are all even. Go ahead and sharpen the tines to a point. It is much easier to do this now than when the rake is assembled. Clean off the top side of the head with a block plane or spokeshave to bring any protruding tine ends level with the surface.

Assembly

The head must now be bored to take the handle and the bows. Find the center of the head on one side by referring to the center mark on the bottom. On both sides of this center line, bore a 1/2-inch hole clear through the head. The two holes should be canted back toward the teeth at about 5° off of perpendicular, closing up the angle between the stail and the head to prevent the

rake from chattering and jumping in use. Using a 1/2-inch chisel, cut out the space between the two holes to leave the 1-by-1/2-inch slot where the stail will fit through the head. Bore the 1/4-inch holes for the bows and the head is ready.

Prepare the stail by cutting the end down to fit snugly through the slot in the head. To find the locations for the bow holes in the stail, lay it alongside the head with its end even with the slot in the head. Transfer the locations of the bow holes in

Bore the 1/4-inch holes for the bows and the center hole for the stail through the head.

Taper the end of the stail to fit through the hole in the head and bore the holes for the bows to pass through it.

the head to the stail, and the bows will form perfect semicircles when assembled.

Put the bows through the holes in the stail and thread them into their proper places in the head. Knock the head on, making sure that the stail is coming in from the correct side of the angled hole.

The last piece to go in is the center tine. With the stail firmly in place, bore a 7/16-inch hole through the head and stail. Drive the last tine in, even it up, and sharpen it down.

Brad through both the head and the stail to secure the bows into their final positions, and you're done.

Bore the last hole through the head and the stail, set in the last tine to lock them together, and plane the top off smooth. Secure the bows into position with brads or wedges.

The Rake's Progress—a load going to market.

Chapter 6. Chairs

Dreaming of a return to Pine Mountain was escape and perhaps death,
but building chairs was adjustment and regeneration.
—Michael Owen Jones, *The Hand Made Object and Its Maker* (1975)

With five tools—an axe, a draw-knife, a shaving horse, an auger, and a chisel—you can turn trees into chairs. Post-and-rung or "stick" chairs are simple and satisfying to make. During bad economic times their simplicity of construction makes them an easy item for country folk to produce and sell. During better times the satisfaction of making your own chair is reward enough.

What sort of chair are you going to make? Certainly you want one that fits and pleases you. I will give instructions here for a small, low rocker, but it's best to find a chair that you like, set it beside you, and copy it as you work. Nothing is quite so good as having a pattern close at hand. After a copy job or two you'll be ready to try one freestyle with confidence.

When you sit down, you don't want to have any doubts about what you're sitting on. To a great extent, the tightness of the woven seat pulled even tighter by your sitting on it is what keeps the chair together. When you lean back, though, the chair is prevented from coming apart, or "racking," only by the security of the bond between each post and rung. As it was in making rakes, part of the secret of strength is to use differential shrinkage to bond the joints together. Everywhere that one of the rungs (horizontal) goes into a post (vertical) the former should be bone dry and the latter still somewhat green so that the joint will age itself tight.

Any reasonably strong wood that will split straight will make a good chair. Too soft a wood, such as white pine, will not be able to stand the compression on the cross grain of the tenon ends of the rungs, and the joints will fail. I have seen strange country chairs out of woods like red

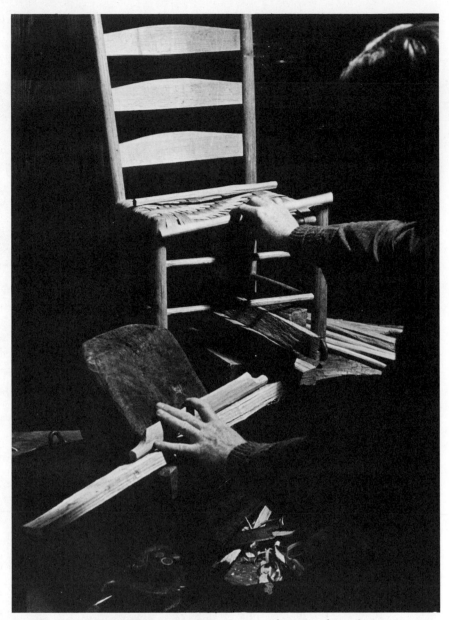

Set the chair that you want to copy next to you and start making the pieces.

mulberry, but many of them were in pieces because the wood lacked the necessary compressive strength. To some extent, you can compensate for weak wood by spreading the load in larger joints. The weaker the wood, the larger the size of the mortice and tenon joints that you must use. One last thing to remember is never to whistle when you go to cut wood for a rocking chair, for

if you do, your chair will squeak when you rock.

Rungs, Splats, and Rockers

Make the parts that need to be driest—the rungs—first. Split them from a block of straight-grained wood that is as long as the longest

Riving white oak for chair splats

Inside the shop

A cutting gauge and a panel-raising plane

Trimming splats with a bow saw

rung—about fifteen inches on my chair. Woven-seat chairs use two kinds of rungs: the regular round ones and the four odd ones that frame the seat weaving. These four seat rungs are wing shaped in cross-section to enable them to support you without breaking. When you have split out the blanks for all these rungs, rough them down with a drawknife to about 20 per-cent larger than their finished size (5/8 inch in diameter on my chair) and put them aside to dry. The final shaping and smoothing can be done only when you're sure that the shrinkage of these pieces is complete.

When the rungs are put away, begin splitting out the back splats. The splats on my chair are about 12 1/2 inches long and 1/4 inch thick; I rive them out of green wood, just as I would roof shingles. Most woods for chairs, like oak and walnut, want to split radially rather than tangen-tially: that is, across the growth rings,

like the spokes of a wheel, rather than with the rings. The best way to find out how the wood you are working with will split is, again, to experiment. You should try to divide the wood exactly in half each time. Don't try to split a piece into thirds, because you must put the same bending stress on both halves of the piece being split. If one of the halves is thinner and is bent more than the other, the fibers on that half will be stressed and weakened more than those on the other and the split will run out that way. You can control the direction of the split to some extent by putting extra stress on the thick side by bending it more than usual.

The splats for the back must be curved. Take the riven-out splats and shave them thin and smooth so that they will bend evenly. If they are still green, you can bend them as they are and they will hold the set. Drier stock will need to be steamed for about an hour. Bend the splats by weaving them between three poles,

as you used to do with popsicle sticks. Pieces this thin will be set in a few days, but a week is best.

If your chair is to have rockers, rive the pieces for them out of the same straight stock used for the splats. As long as the wood is split out and not sawed, the rockers can be as thin as 3/8 inch and still be plenty strong; however, rockers that thin may be hard on rugs. Trace the pattern of one of the rockers of your copy chair onto the blanks. The outside, or convex, curve is easily cut to the line with the axe; the inside, however, will need a single saw or axe cut to the bottom of the curve so that a split started at one end won't run out through the rocker at the other end. Cut down from the ends into the middle of the rocker with a double-beveled hand axe to within 1/8 inch of the line. When both are roughed out, clamp them together and shave them as one with the spokeshave. Put them away to dry.

Rive the splats for the back from straight, green stock.

If one side of the split starts to get thicker than the other, bending it extra hard will cause the split to run back.

Set the splats up like this and they will all be bent evenly. They should be set in a week or so.

Posts

The short front posts are simple, as they are short and straight. The back, main posts, though, are usually curved so that you don't have to sit bolt upright. It's best to use a small bent tree that can be split into two equally curved pieces. An alternative is to bend straight green pieces by tying the ends together with a block in the middle to get an equal bend on them both. The problem with this method is getting back posts dry enough to hold the bend, yet green enough to season shut around the rung tenons. Usually, it works out all right, but you must remember to balance these two factors.

The posts should be worked to

Chop out the rockers from split stock. The bevel of the hatchet must be on the concave side of the work—in this case, to my left.

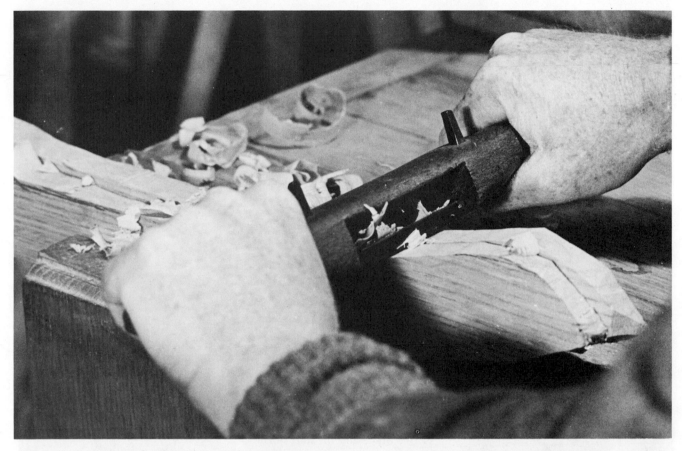

Clamp the two rough rockers in the vise and shave them as one.

their final shape as soon as possible. As you did with the rockers, you can clamp the curved back posts together and plane or shave them as one. Most posts are round, so you can proceed to shave them octagonal and then to full round, or you can just leave them square.

A bit of lathe work on the top of the back posts can be added here. This is an easy step if you are using straight stock that you intend to bend. Just put the green stock in the lathe and turn the finials, and then set them up to bend. Even with turned finials on the posts, however, I do all the rounding of the length of the posts with shaves and planes. Few things are as tiresome to me as turning a 4-foot-long cylinder on a foot-operated lathe.

The two back posts may be bent equally by trussing them with a spacer block in between.

Assembly—
One Half at a Time

When you're ready to put it all together, the rungs, splats, and rockers should all be dry, the four posts still somewhat green. Assemble the two sides of the chair first, then join these two halves with the seat splayed out in the front as it should be, spring in the splats, and put on the rockers.

Bring all your rungs down to their finished size. A small hollow-bottomed plane will give you an excellent finish on the dry wood, but you can do quite well with simply a drawknife and shave. You may wish to have the rungs slightly larger in their midsections than on the ends. Shape a slightly oversized tenon to fit a 5/8-inch-diameter hole on one end of each of the rungs with the drawknife. With experience,

When the rungs are dry, the tenons (the parts that fit into the posts) must be brought to their final size. Here you can see the slight undercutting that creates the "ball" of the ball and socket joint.

you can do this by eye, but you may want to bore a hole in a piece of scrap to use for a guide in the beginning. Be sure to make them somewhat oval so that the stress will be exerted along the grain of the posts. A slight undercutting all the way around the tenon about 1/2 inch back from its end will add much to the strength of the seasoned joints. Remember that the wood of the unseasoned posts is going to shrink up across the grain (horizontal) and not along it (vertical). You must cut the tenon on the rung large enough so that the hole in the post will shrink up tight around it, but not so tight that you crack the post open. Experience alone will teach.

Lay the posts beside one another and scribe the lines where the rungs will be set in. The front and back wing-shaped seat rungs are set in just below the two side seat rungs. This, of course, makes the seat fit your bottom better and keeps your legs from going to sleep.

With a brace and bit start boring the holes for the side rungs in one of the posts. To judge the depth, count the number of turns of the brace that it takes to get to where you want, which is about three-quarters of the way through the post. Stop every five or so turns after shavings appear and see how deep the hole is. The total number of turns that it takes to bring the hole to the right depth will be the number of turns to use on each of the other holes.

Once the first hole is bored, go ahead and drive in the finished tenon of the rung. The wing-shaped seat rung goes in with the trailing edge to the inside of the seat. Having one of the rungs in place will assist you in aligning the next one. Eyeball the brace and bit as you drill to make sure you are lined up with the rung you just put in.

Lay out all four posts and scribe the locations for the rungs all at once.

Get the first rung in straight and square and use it as a guide in boring the rest of the holes. Be sure you will have room to swing the brace and bit, though.

Now you have a post with several rungs sticking out of it. Bore the other post for that side, cut the rungs to length (12 1/2 inches long on my chair), prepare their tenons, and drive it together. You now have either a right- or a left-hand chair half. Go ahead and put together the other half, making sure that the wing shape of the seat rung trails to what will be the inside of the chair.

Another view of the ball and socket.

Joining the Halves

With these two completed halves you can get a good picture of what the chair will look like. Set them up side by side with the splay in the front just as you want it to be in the completed chair. You need to do this in order to judge the angles for boring the holes for the front and back rungs. Now lay one of the chair halves flat on the floor with the side to be bored facing up. Set the point of the auger on the post where the rung will go and tilt the auger

Cut the rungs to length, shape their tenons, and drive on the other post.

over until you have the angle that you want. As you begin to bore this first hole, sight down over the edge of the top knob of the brace and see what point on the post lies directly below that edge. If you have a well-developed sense of the vertical, you should be able to duplicate this angle on all of the remaining holes by tilting the brace over until you see this same relative point. Drive in the first rung when you have bored its hole and it will serve as an additional guide in getting the rest of the holes correctly angled.

When all the rungs are set in one side, stand up the two sides together in another mock assembly. Move them about until you have it just the way you want it to be and then mark all the rungs where they must be cut off. Set the two halves back down again, saw the rungs to length, and shape the tenons on their ends. Use mock assemblies to check your angles as you bore all of the holes in the second half. When the holes are done, you can drive the two halves together.

Clamp the bent splats together and plane their bottom edges. To avoid making a chair that has a top-heavy look, cut the splats progressively narrower from bottom to top. Before you shape the tops of the splats with their arches or whatever, lay the chair down on its back with the splats underneath their proper places. Scribe down the insides of the two back posts onto the splats to mark how long each needs to be. Shape the tops between these lines and leave enough extra on each end to fit into the posts (5/8 inch or so) before you cut them off. Hold the splat in place to judge the angle needed to match its curvature and start morticing. The chisel should, of course, match the width of the splat, about 1/4 inch. At each end of the mortice cut straight in with the flat side of the chisel against what will be the end walls of the mortice. Alternate these chopping cuts with digging cuts, the bevel of the chisel down, until you reach the depth you need. Resist the temptation to use the chisel as a lever against the ends of the mortice.

With everything morticed, spring in the splats. You can bore some tiny peg holes through the posts and splats to keep them tight. Usually only the top splat needs this; the others are allowed to give in and out.

The rockers are attached with bridle joints, chiseled slots in the bottoms of the posts which fit over the rockers. Secure the rockers with 1/4-inch pegs through these joints, but check first to be sure that the chair sits right before you do this. You can adjust the way the chair sits by cutting the slots deeper on the front or back posts.

Test out the chair very carefully. I once had a woman try out a walnut arm rocker that I was making for her. She exceeded the limits of caution,

Stand up the two halves beside one
another in the way you want the chair to
look. Memorize the angle between them.

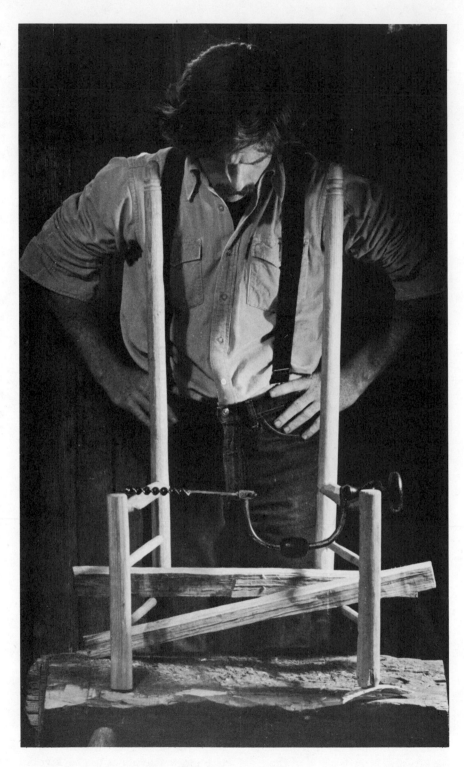

The front and back rungs intersect the
lower quarter of the side rungs and lock
them into place.

Set the auger straight up and down and then tilt it until you can sight down over
the edge of the top handle of the brace and see the edge of the bit. This is usually the
proper angle for my chairs.

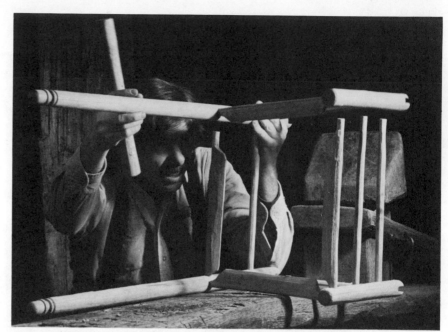

Drive all the rungs into one half of the chair, bore the other half, and put the two together.

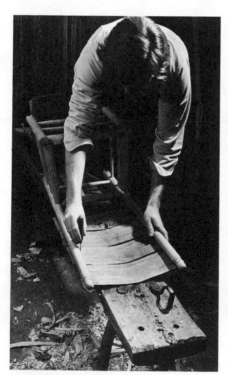

Set the bent splats under the back posts and scribe their lengths.

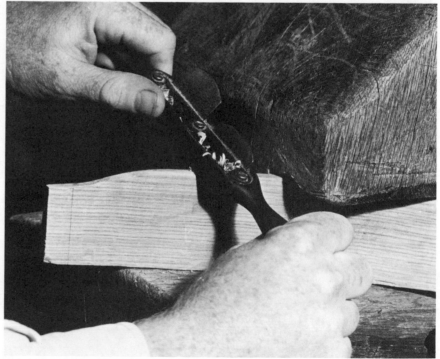

Shape the splats to the pattern you have chosen and cut them to the proper lengths.

Cut slots for the splats, matching their angle carefully. Chop down at both ends of the slot and dig out the wood in between.

Spring in the splats.

Peg your rockers well.

and the chair came off the unpegged rockers, depositing her on her back. Helping her and the chair back into standing position, I laughed and lectured her on the need to be careful when test fitting rockers. Not satisfied with verbally correcting her approach to this delicate procedure, I put the chair back on its rockers, sat down, took one rock back, and immediately pitched over backward myself, hitting my head on the woodstove. She was still laughing when I regained consciousness.

Chapter 7. Weaving Wood

Other crafts employ oak as a pliant material for weaving
baskets or wattle hurdles.
—H. L. Edlin, *Woodland Crafts in Britain* (1949)

That's an excellent chair you just
made. So now to put a bottom in it.
Lots of different kinds of materials
can be woven into a comfortable
chair seat: cattails, torn cottonmill
rovings, corn shucks, elm or hickory
bark, rawhide. I work mostly with
splits ("splints," in the North) made
from the sapwood of white oak, and
that's what this chapter is about: how
to make the splits, how to weave the

chair bottoms, and how to make a
melon basket.

The Splitting Tree

First, find a suitable tree. You should
look for a white oak, any one of
several species of oak without bristle
tips on the ends of the veins in the

*Basket maker Bryant Holsenbeck works
on a melon or egg basket while I put in
another chair bottom.*

The bark on this small white oak is clear and straight, but somewhat coarse. It's probably a good enough tree for chair bottoms, but marginal for finer baskets.

A professional basket maker's stash of white oak. These 6-to-8-inch-diameter logs will still be good for making splits even after several months of lying in the open. White oak dries very slowly when left whole with the bark on.

leaves. Find one with soft, straight, smooth, even bark. It should be about 3 to 8 inches in diameter and have this perfect bark for as long a length as possible. Only the section with good bark can be expected to have good wood, so this is the limit on how long the individual splits can be.

You can hear lots of tales about where to look for good splitting trees. I'm not so sure that what works on one mountain will work in the next valley. Some of the variation between trees may be genetic rather than environmental. Growth rate may or may not affect how a particular tree will split. The only thing to do is to see what works in your woods. That's the fun of it.

Old-time basket makers often chopped a chunk out of the base of a tree to see if it split well. If it didn't look good, they left the tree standing. I don't approve of this practice, but it has led to at least one good story, told to me by Lew LeCompte, whose cooperage business takes him to the woods quite often.

"We were out in the woods with old Mr. Kyle getting some white oak for his baskets and he was cutting into this tree with his axe to check the grain to see if it was good stuff or not. He was cutting in there and he hits this rotten spot in the heart. All of a sudden he drops down on his knees and puts his hand over the rotten spot and starts yelling for someone to get him a match. I had some matches and he says hurry and light one and give it to him. He takes that match and holds it to the cut in the tree and this long clear flame starts shooting out of the notch like a blowtorch. There was some kind of gas coming out of the tree and I mean it was burning hot, just like a blowtorch. We just stood there and stared at that flame for about a minute before it turned yellow and went out with a 'pop.' Mr. Kyle looked up at the two of us standing there with our mouths hanging open and he says, 'What'sa matter, fellers? Ain't you ever seen anybody light one before?'"

Making Splits

Once the usable length of tree is back at the shop, start splitting it up. The part you're interested in is the white sapwood. Split off the heart as close as you can to the dividing line between the light and dark wood. You don't really need to do it, but I always shave off the bark and any remaining heart. I work it down until I have a piece of clean sapwood that is as wide in the plane of the growth rings as I want the splits to be—say, 1 inch for chair bottoms—and as thick as the sapwood was on the tree.

Now comes the proof of the matter. Take the blade of a jackknife and set it in the exact middle of the end of the piece in the same line as the growth rings. Drive the blade in with a stick to start the split. Once the split is started, work it down the rest of the way with your hands. Keep the split centered by putting more bend into the thicker side. This bend will further stress and weaken the fibers on the thick side and make the split run back that way.

Continue splitting each piece in half, with the growth rings, until they are as thin as you want or can achieve. Don't give up if it doesn't work at first. Quite often the wood on one side of a tree will not work at all, while that on the other side does just fine. There is almost as much variation within a single tree as there is between different trees.

Once you have broken the log open with the froe, the wood begins to dry more rapidly. The first split will usually tell you if you have chosen the right tree. This tree has a generous proportion of sapwood for making splits.

Continue splitting each piece exactly in half into pie-shaped sections by starting each split with the froe and continuing it in the manner shown here.

From now on, make all splits in the same plane as the annual growth rings. This small froe is made from an old automobile leaf spring.

Continue the split down the length of the piece. Keep the split centered by bending the thicker side more sharply.

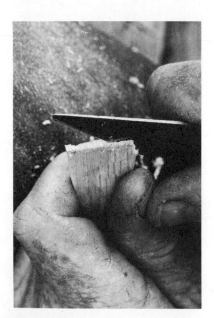

When they get small enough, start your splits by working in a knife from the corner.

If you can't split all the wood right away, leave the log in a shady spot or even in a pond until you can get back to it. I've made excellent splits from logs that lay on the north side of the shop for as long as three months.

When you finish preparing the splits, gather them up and set them aside to dry. If you were to weave them now, they would shrink in width so much upon drying that even the tightest work would loosen up.

After the splits have dried a bit, you can shave them smoother by drawing them between your knee and a knife held vertical to their surface. If the splits are wider than you want, you can cut them to any width with a pair of regular scissors.

When the time comes to use them, don't soak them in water or you will get the same kind of shrinking problem. All you need to do is dip them for a minute or so; then they do quite well.

Chair Bottoming

The woven seat is made by wrapping the splits around the front and back seat rungs (the warp) and then interweaving as you wrap around from side to side (the woof). I wrap the front to back part first because the front edge of the seat is what will be seen the most. Since it is the most visible, you want it to be the tightest: that is, you don't want gaps to show between the splits. It's much easier to get the warp splits to sit close together than it is to get the woof splits tight. Start in the front corner by putting the end of your first split underneath the front rung and tacking or catching its end on the side rung. Bring the free end up around the front and take it over the top of the seat and around the back. Pull tight each time you go around.

When you reach the end of this split, you will need to splice in

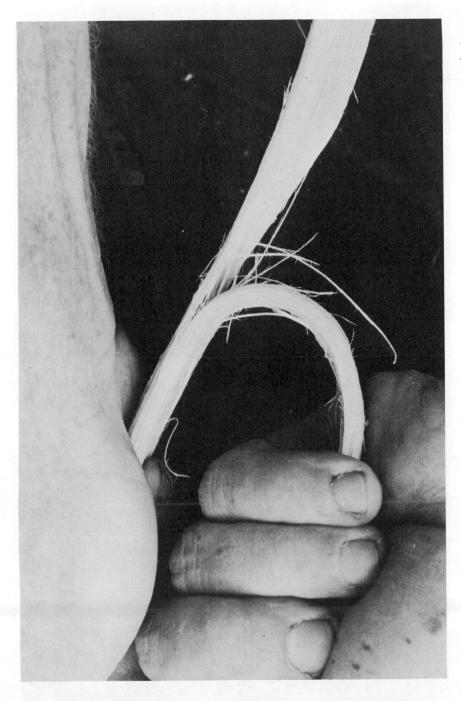

In the event of severe "run out," hold the piece below the split with one hand and pull the thick side sharply back on itself to bring the split back into line.

another. All the splices should end up on the underside of the seat. It's painful, but when a split is not long enough to reach back around and make the splice underneath, you'll have to cut it shorter.

Depending on how "pure" you want your chair to be, you can choose one of two kinds of splices.

If you didn't use tacks to hold the end of the first split in place, then you ought to use the hook-and-eye splice. If you did use tacks, then you shouldn't feel bad about using thread to do tie splices.

To make tie splices, cut in notches on the sides of both splits, wrap heavy thread around, and tie it up.

These splices are very strong.

To complete the warping, turn down under the corner at the back and come up on the side. Now you are set to begin weaving the woof. If you want to, dye your woof splits in water and walnut hulls for added effect. The plain weave is so simple that you hardly ever see it. You just

Shave the splits smooth—if you wish—by pulling them between your leg and a knife.

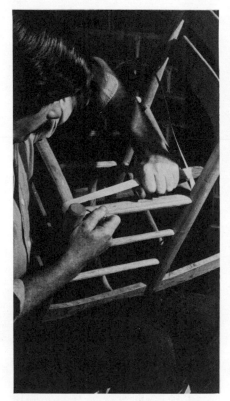

Start the warp of the chair bottom from front to back. The tail end, held down here by my right thumb, will be secured by the side-to-side weaving.

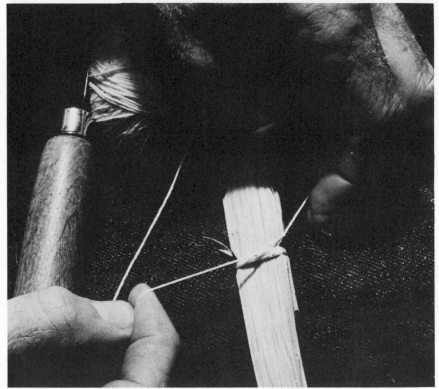

Tied splices are quick and strong, but you need to buy or make string.

Hook-and-Eye Splices

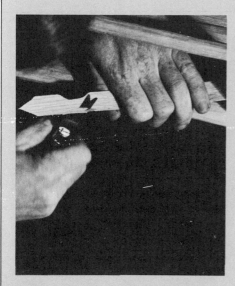 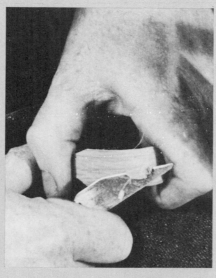 

Hook-and-eye splices are a bit more trouble, but when cleanly done, they look so neat that you could have them on the top side of the seat as well. The hook is easy to cut with a sharp knife.

To make the eye, double over the new split about 2 inches from the end and slice it open across the grain.

A better name for this splice is "lock and key." Once you have made the round opening, finish the keyhole shape of the eye by tearing out a small strip and cutting it off with your knife.

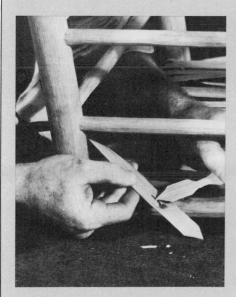 

Put the key into the lock (or the hook into the eye).

Arrange each splice so that the free ends will be on the "inside" of the seat.

When you reach the far back corner from where you began, simply come down and up around on the side to begin the interweaving. For a herringbone weave, go over two, under two and then get out of step by one on the next go-round.

Pull each split tight as you go.

A doubled plain weave on the underside saves having to think.

go over one and under the next and then alternate on the next go-round. The herringbone weave is by far the most popular and just as easy to do. On the first course you go over two and under two all the way across. When you start the second course, you get out of step by going over only one at the start and then under two and over two the rest of the way across. The third course starts by going under two, the fourth by going under one, and the next one starts back at the beginning. Do the bottom side in doubled plain weave to save time.

Each run must be pulled as tight as possible and pushed up against the preceding split. When you get toward the front you'll find the warp splits getting very tight and you may have to use a stick to pry open the space to push the last splits through. When you get to the end of the last run, weave the loose end underneath, double it back and tuck it under, and sit down.

This old chair bottom shows no concern for even widths, but is still in her-ringbone weave and stuffed with shav-ings and pine needles. The basket is made of the same material as the chair bottom, but with seven times more care. The "eyes" that join the two hoops that frame this basket are quite distinctive.

Beat each course up tight to the one before it.

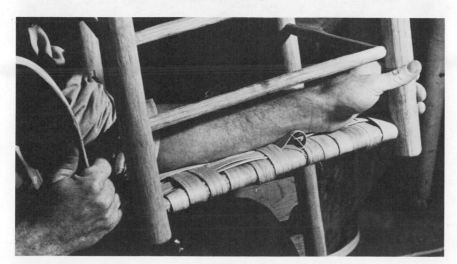

Finish up by doubling back on the last split on the underside.

A Melon Basket

White-oak baskets come in many variations. I will show you a moderately complex one known as a melon or gizzard basket.

The handle and rim of this basket are formed by two hoops set into each other at right angles. The intersections of the hoops are joined by lashings called "eyes." These two eyes also hold the ends of the initial ribs that are added to form the rest of the frame. Within this framework of ribs and hoops narrow splits, or "weavers," are interwoven to complete the body of the basket.

The hoops are relatively heavy splits about 1/8 inch thick and about 1 inch wide. These hoops are joined with hook-and-eye splices with the free ends put to the inside. The size of these hoops determines the size of the basket, so that is up to you.

Lash the two hoops together with a very thin and narrow length of split. The pattern that you use for the eye is often your trademark, so beyond the sequence shown here I'll leave you to discover your own. Leave the ends of the eye lashings long, as they will be used to hold the ribs in place.

Whittle the ribs from heartwood, 1/8 inch in diameter for small baskets, 1/4 inch for larger ones. Sharpen the ends of four ribs and stick them into one of the eyes as best you can, two on each side of the hoop. You can put in more ribs for larger or finer baskets; just make sure to use equal numbers, on both sides of the hoop. Take the end of the eye strip and weave it in and out of the ribs and hoops until the ribs are firmly held in place.

Now go to the other end of the basket and bend over the ribs to meet the other eye in the shape that you want the basket to take. Cut the excess length off the ends and

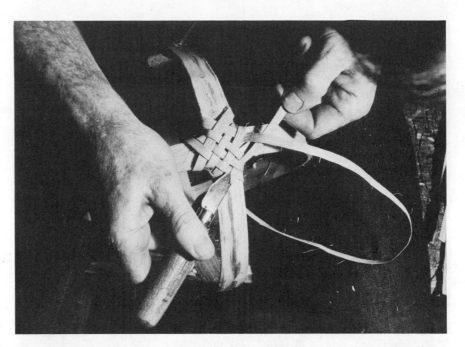

The two hoops that frame this egg basket are joined to themselves with hook-and-eye splices. Set one hoop inside the other and lash their intersection with long, narrow strips woven into "eyes." The pattern that I use goes around each arm, comes back around under itself, and then on to the next. Leave the long end of the strip attached.

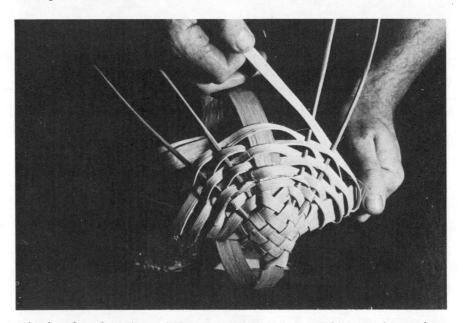

Whittle at least four 1/8-to-3/16-inch ribs from the heartwood left over from making the splits. The larger and finer the basket, the more ribs you will need. Point the ends of the ribs and stick them into the eye on the side that will be to the bottom. Put half the ribs on one side and half on the other side of the hoop that will form the keel of the basket. Take the end of the eye strip and start to weave in and out. This locks the ribs in place.

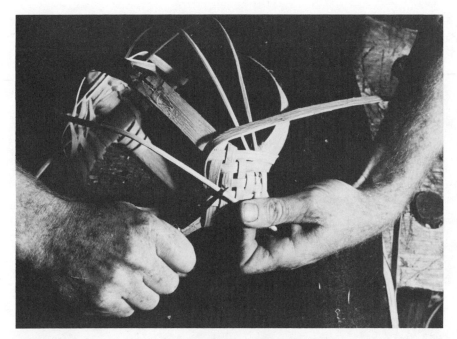

sharpen them so that you can stick them into this eye just like you did before. Lock these ends down with the length from the eye weaving and the beginning frame is ready.

Take a long, thin split and tuck it in to take up where the extra from the eye left off. Continue weaving along until this split runs out and then start back on the other end. You don't need to splice each added piece, just overlap.

Weave toward the middle from both ends until you feel the need to add more ribs. Stick these down into the previous weaving and then carry on. Your weaving will meet in the middle and you're all done.

Weave an eye on the other side if you have not done so already. Bend the ribs over into the shape that you want the basket to take. Point them and stick them in the second eye as before. Do the same sort of weaving on this side as you did on the other.

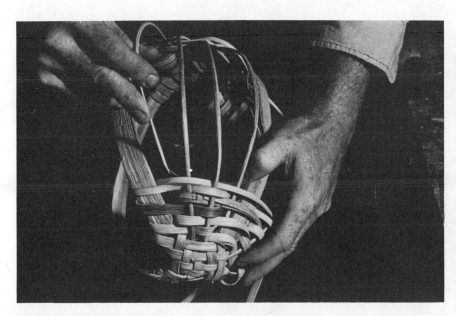

When you feel the need to do so, add more ribs evenly to both sides by just sticking them into the weaving as best you can.

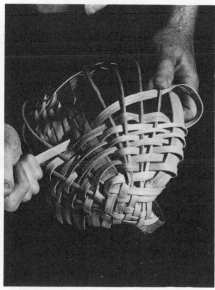

Continue weaving the two ends toward one another. When a strip runs out, simply lap another in on top of it—no splice, just overlap. The two sides will meet in the middle, and there's your basket.

Chapter 8. Hay Forks

A pitch-fork, a dung-fork, sieve, skep and a bin,
a broom, and a pail, to put water therin;
—Thomas Tusser, *Five Hundred Points of Husbandry* (1557)

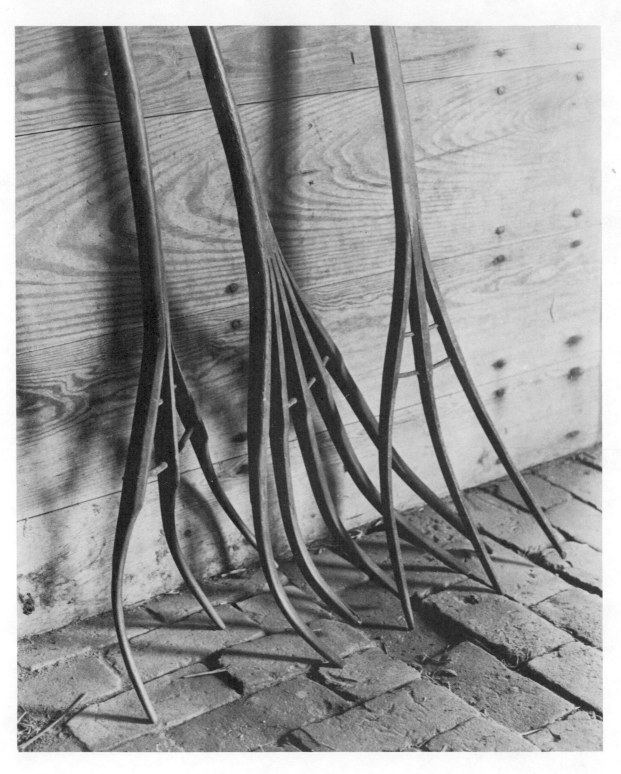

People seem to have a special fascination with hay forks. It's easy to see why. The classic cyma curve of the handle leads the eye down to the diverging paths of the tines and the realization that it is all of one piece of wood. Making these forks is excellent winter work. The bending process requires steam, so you have a good excuse to hover near the potbellied stove, stoking the fire with the piles of shavings produced.

Splitting Out the Billet

Start with only the very best wood you can find. The bending process will discover any weak spot in the grain and cause the fork to break right there, so choose carefully. I look for about 8-inch-diameter ash, hickory, or white oak that has straight, even bark and is clear of knots.

Cut a 6-foot length and start splitting. You should end up with a billet that runs at least 1 by 2 inches the full length of the piece. Be careful that the flat faces of the billet are oriented either in line with or at right angles to the growth rings. If the rings run diagonally through the cross-section of the fork, it will tend to bend unevenly.

Shaping the Blank

At the shaving horse, shape the billet down as follows. This is for a light-duty, three-tine fork. You may, of course, beef up the pattern and add more tines if you wish, but this is a good way to start. You can do the measuring with one of the two folding cubit rules that you were issued at birth. The distance from your elbow to your wrist (two-thirds

Straight-grained ash makes excellent forks.

Shape the blank with the drawknife.

Finish up with the spokeshave. The thin part goes from elbow to wrist; the thick part from wrist to fingertip.

of a cubit) is the length for the narrow part of the tines; make this section 1 1/2 inches wide and 1/2 inch thick. The wide part of the tines where the spreader rods will go should be the same distance as from your wrist to your fingertips (one-third of a cubit); make this part 1 1/2 inches wide and 1 inch thick. The drawknife and spokeshave are the main tools for shaping, but don't forget the hollow-bottomed fork-staff plane from chapter 5. This is the job that gave it its name.

Preparing the Head

Once the fork has been shaped, you can bore the holes for the 1/4-inch hickory rods, or spreaders, that hold the tines apart. Bore these three holes through the fork at the locations shown. It is best to bore these holes now, before you saw the tines apart. If you wait to do this after the

sawing, you will leave raggedy places between the tines that will be hard to clean up later.

Since this is a three-tined fork, you need to divide the width of the blank into thirds. Draw guidelines and saw right down them. Be careful not to twist the saw to the sides as you cut, as you may cause a split to run where you don't want it to. If the grain of your blank is perfect and you want to take the chance, you can do all the tine separating by splitting.

To prevent the accidental creation of three one-tined forks, you must rivet the head of the fork together just below the point where the tines diverge from the handle. Use a nail through the shaft and peen its sawn-off end over a small washer. You will probably need to bore the hole for this nail in order to prevent it from splitting the handle when you drive it through. Here, a word of caution. When you drill through unseasoned wood with a small bit, the flutes of the bit will choke and pack very

quickly. If you drill into the fork until the drill packs up and then try to turn it out backward, you will wedge the bit and break it off in the wood. Always drill a short ways in and then pull out while still cranking forward to clear the bit before continuing. This goes for large bits as well. Alternatively, burn the hole through with a red-hot iron rod.

Steaming and Bending

Once the work has been shaped, bored, sawed, and riveted, you're ready to get up steam. My favorite rig for this job is a steam box made from a T section of a 6-inch stovepipe set over an old pot. The advantage of this unit is that you can adjust its length to suit the job by adding or subtracting sections of pipe. What would really make it nice would be to add a whistle. Maybe next year.

You can also make up a steam box from some boards and a pot, or just dip the fork in boiling water. Or you can do as they used to do in eastern Europe and bury your forks in fresh, hot manure for a few weeks. I haven't tried this last one yet.

Spread the tines of the fork apart with some small blocks of wood to let the steam get in. When the pot is boiling, set in the fork and stuff the end of the steam box with rags. It needs to cook for an hour.

While the fork is steaming (if not before), you should rig up a bending jig of some sort. The strongest and simplest jig is made from two reject shingles (heavy ones) or boards and four 1-inch-thick oak rods. Take one of the shingles and draw on its side the bend that you want the fork to take. Clamp the two shingles together and bore 1-inch holes through them both at the apex of each curve. Bore the holes so that

Bore the three holes for the spreaders.

Saw the tines apart.

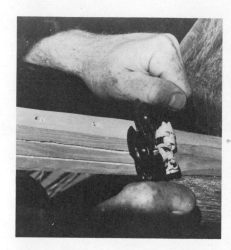

Reshave the sides to equalize any error from sawing. All must bend equally.

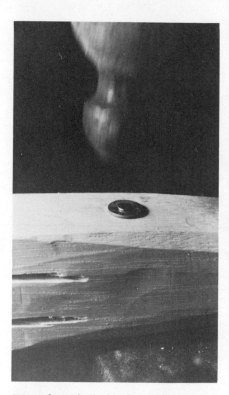

Rivet through the head just below the saw cuts.

The stovepipe steamer on the potbelly stove.

Put the hot fork in the frame. One more peg goes in at the top. Separator blocks are just visible behind the second peg from the bottom.

they are on the outside side of each curve to give you more bend than you want in the finished fork. This will give you some allowance for springback.

The up-and-down bend of the fork is determined by the position of the holes in the shingles. The tines must also be bent out to the sides to the desired spread. To hold the tines apart, use two nails driven into each of the two rods that will bend the tip end of the fork. Drive these nails into the rods at 5 or 6 inches on either side of their midpoints. If you prefer, you can forget the nails and spread the tines by driving blocks of wood between them when they go into the frame.

When the fork has steamed for an hour, get the jig ready with the two nailed rods in place. Take the fork out and set the tips of the tines on the first rod. Pull the tines apart and push the fork against the second rod so that the tines catch on the outside of its two nails. The tines should now be on the inside of the two nails on the first rod and on the outside of the nails on the second rod. This overbends the tines slightly pigeon-toed so that they will point straight ahead when they spring back.

Now bend the body of the fork over and put in the third rod, bend it back again and put in the fourth rod. Check to see that everything is aligned properly and knock it around until you feel it's right.

Forget about it for a week.

Final Steps

Depending on the moisture content of the wood, seven to fourteen days should be enough time for it to set up. You can tell by weight and feel how dry the wood is. If you have any doubts, let it rest longer.

When it's set, and you're sure it's set, take it out of the jig and finish it up. The middle tine will be longer than the outside ones because it goes straight to the end. Cut it off even with the others. Clean up and round the tines with a spokeshave. Get some lengths of 1/4-inch hickory or other rods and put them through the holes that you bored for them. Carefully spread the tines apart so that they look the way you want them to. Get some long thin brads (beekeepers usually have nails of this size) and nail down through the tines into each intersection with the spreader rods.

Go look for some hay.

After it has been in the frame a week or so, take it out and shave it down.

Put the spreader rods through and brad them in place.

Chapter 9. Dough Bowls

A short saw, and long saw, to cut a-two logs,
an axe, and an adze, to make trough for thy hogs;
—Thomas Tusser, *Five Hundred Points of Husbandry* (1557)

From spoons to dugout canoes, the manufacture of wooden articles by hollowing is one of the oldest woodworking trades. We're all familiar with pictures of native Americans hollowing out canoes by charring the wood with a small fire and cleaning it up with a shell, stone, or bone adz. With steel tools, burning is no longer necessary, but the careful judgment required to gauge the evenness of the hollowing remains the same.

Hewn wooden bowls are good to make. These long dough bowls or bread trays never fail to please. They're beautiful, and when not in use for bread making, provide a home for apples and oranges. As with anything associated with food, they have a universal appeal.

Tulip poplar is easy to work and splits easily into the blanks for hollowing out.

Roughing Out the Blank

Almost any wood can be used for hollowware, depending upon what purpose the piece is to serve. Food containers should be made from an easily worked wood that will impart no taste of its own, for example, maple, black gum, basswood, sycamore, or elm. I usually use tulip poplar both because it is readily available to me and because it is easy to work. Soft and easily split when green (sometimes too easily), it shapes nicely with the axe and adz. In addition, it takes a good finish and resists unwanted splitting well enough when it dries.

The splitting characteristics of the wood are important, for this is how you will prepare the rough blank from which to hew the bowl. You don't want to incorporate the heart (the first-year growth ring of the log) into the body of the bowl, because checks will certainly appear around this point. For this reason the bowl is hewn from the long-grain half of

Chop out notches with the single-beveled hatchet on either end of the area to be hollowed out and then split out the wood in between. Continue notching and splitting out with the hatchet until you approach the size you want.

a split log. The hollow of the bowl is cut out of the heart-side face; the bottom is the bark side.

Cut a green log to the length that you want the bowl to be and split it in half. Do this before any seasoning checks appear in the end grain and ruin the bowl before you've begun. You may have to use a piece out of the midsection of the log if it has been down very long. Decide how deep you want the bowl to be and split off enough of the bark side to leave you with a suitable blank. About 3 or 4 inches is good for a start. You don't want to find that you've split off more than you can hew.

Hollowing Out

Even up the top and bottom faces with your hatchet. You may want to draw the outline of the hollow that you are going to make on the top of the blank, or you can do as I do and just chop it all out by eye. Begin the actual hollowing by roughing out the inside of the bowl. Using the hewing hatchet, you can make this go very fast. Chop out a notch across the grain on both ends of the space that you're going to hollow out. Having made these two notches, you can safely split out the wood in between without the risk of breaking open the ends of the bowl. When you have split out all that the first notches will allow, cut deeper notches and continue splitting until you've gone as deep as you need.

All of this chopping and splitting should be done with the bevel of the hewing hatchet down against the work. This means that as you work, you need to keep turning the work end for end so that the bevel stays down. You always want to keep the cutting edge of the hatchet leading

Follow the axe work with a bowl adz.

A long, two-handed version like this one may also be used. You can reforge a garden mattock to make one.

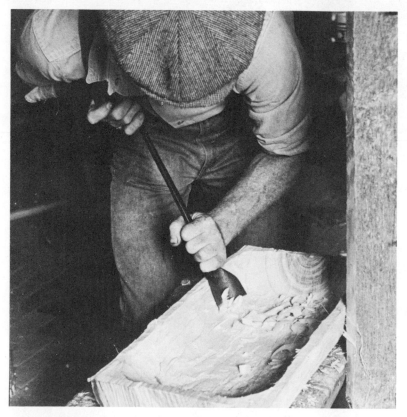

Clean up the inside with a gouge. This one has a T handle on it to let you put on shoulder pressure.

to the inside of the hollow being created.

The hand axe works fast, but does not adapt well to smoothing out the inside. For this you need a gouge of some sort, either a mallet-driven one or an impact tool, such as the bowl adz. A bowl adz resembles a regular adz except that it is curved, both across the cutting edge and along the length of the head. Bowl adzes come in both single-handed and two-handed versions. The handle on a two-handed bowl adz is only about two feet long to keep the radius of the swing tighter than a longer handle would permit.

Don't confuse a bowl adz with a gutter adz. Gutter adzes are curved across the cutting edge but straight along their length. They are made primarily for hewing the long open troughs of wooden rain gutters. Gutter adzes have too long a turning radius and will dig in every time in bowl work. Some manufacturers know this and forge them thick enough to allow regrinding with the bevel out. This makes them satisfactory for bowl hewing. It used to be the same way with axe heads. They were sold forged very blunt because the manufacturer could not know if you wanted the axe for splitting or for chopping. He would leave it to you to grind it down if you wanted it for the latter.

With adz or mallet-driven gouge, begin cutting and smoothing the interior of the bowl to its final contour. The shallower the slope on the ends, the easier the work will be. Bring everything down even, but don't try to remove every tool mark yet for a finished surface. Before you do that, you'll want to shape the outside. The inside smoothing is tedious in the extreme, and since you stand a chance of cracking the bowl in the process of shaping the outside, it is generally better to wait to smooth the interior until you're more sure of success.

The bulk of the wood on the exterior can be removed with the hand axe. Most of the work will be in shaping the slope on the ends of the bowl, where the wood is weakest. Hold the bowl so that the surface to be created is vertical and cut down with the flat side of the hatchet against the bulk of the wood. Be sure that the rim of the bowl directly below where you are cutting is well supported. Stress caused by chopping over hollows in the cutting block is one of the leading causes of cracked dough bowls.

Once the outside has been roughed out with the axe, you may find that you are able to hold it in the shaving horse and finish smoothing it off with the drawknife. This works extraordinarily well when the wood is still soft and green. Or sit on the overturned bowl and smooth it off by pushing down away from you with a spokeshave, set rank to remove healthy shavings.

The success of the bowl is measured in large part by how even you get its thickness at every point. Try to judge its thickness or thinness at a given point by tapping it with a stick of wood and listening to the tone.

Drying the Bowl

Checking, or unwanted cracking, can be a problem as the bowl dries out. The ends of the bowl are the end grain of the log, which causes two problems. The end grain is weaker and splits easily anyway, and it loses moisture faster and hence shrinks up faster than the long grain of the sides of the bowl.

You can try to control checking two ways. First, design the bowl so that the end grain is strengthened.

Chop down the outside with the hatchet.

Give the ends of the bowl a long slope or add some handles on each end. Both of these will add length and strength to the end grain. Second, slow down the drying of the bowl so that it will season at a more uniform rate. You can do this in a number of ways: coat the bowl with lard or vegetable oil so that the moisture will escape slowly; selectively wet the end grain with water to give the sides a chance to catch up; or pack the bowl in something like fresh sawdust so that the whole mass will have to dry as one.

I have used all of these procedures at one time or other, but I usually rely on wetting down the problem spots with water. After shaping out the whole bowl in one sitting, I wet the end grain down and then inspect and rewet as necessary for about a month or so until the bowl is dry enough for finishing.

During the drying process the two long sides of the bowl will contract more than the radial grain of the ends. This will cause the middle of the short ends of the bowl to crown up. If you find this or other distortions objectionable, you can level the top of the bowl with a plane or a drawknife and spokeshave.

Smoothing and Sealing

The inside of the bowl still has all of the ridges and furrows of the adz or gouge. Getting this inside completely smooth is a moderately tedious job and has resulted in the creation of some rather peculiar tools. All kinds of curved shaves have been contrived for this job, each with its own problem. Nothing seems to work better, though, than what those fellows with the oyster shells and the fire were doing—scraping.

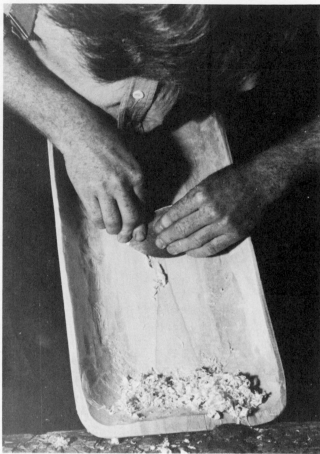

Finish smoothing the outside with the drawknife or spokeshave.   *Finish the interior with a convex scraper.*

Scrapers may not work as well on unseasoned wood, so wait until the bowl is moderately dry if you have problems. You can make a scraper from a broken-off piece of an old crosscut saw or some other hard steel. Grind a curve on one side to fit into the concave bowl. Draw a file along the length of this curve to sharpen it to a perfectly square cutting edge. The square edge of the rounded face does the scraping as you push or pull it across the surface.

If you feel that it is necessary, you can finish up the inside of the bowl by sanding, either with sandpaper or with leather and loose sand.

Use only edible oils to seal the wood of the bowl. Linseed oil is not appropriate. You have to keep putting on oil until the wood is permeated with it. This makes the bowl easier to clean.

Wooden Scoops and Shovels

Using these techniques, you can also make wooden scoops and shovels. Just leave one end open and leave some wood for a handle on the other end. Wooden shovels take about four hours to make. Surprisingly, these shovels still find uses today. They are used for handling foodstuffs where a metal shovel might damage the fruit or grain, and they are also popular with people who handle large quantities of gunpowder, where a spark from a metal shovel could have undesirable effects.

Gunpowder shovels take about four hours to make.

This pull shave is one of hundreds of inventions to smooth the insides of hollowware.

Chapter 10. Three Lathes

But when Turners work heavy Work, such as the Pole and
Tread will not Command, they use the Great Wheel.
—Joseph Moxon, *Mechanick Exercises* (1678)

Remember the endless perfect circles you drew with your compass in grade school geometry class? Even if you couldn't do anything else right, no one could fault you on your circles. With the compass, the potter's wheel, and the turning lathe you are guaranteed that no matter how inexperienced you are, your work will be perfect in at least one plane.

Your encouraging partner in wood turning is the lathe, a machine that imparts rotary motion to the work so that it may be shaped by the steady application of the cutting tool. I use three different lathes in the shop: the elegant spring-pole lathe, the notorious great-wheel lathe, and the sensible treadle lathe. Each of these machines represents a leap of sorts in the development of one aspect of technology: that is, the conversion of reciprocating, or back-and-forth, motion into the true circular motion that gets so many things done today.

The Spring-pole Lathe

The spring-pole lathe was the first of these to be developed. The piece to be turned is held between two conical points called "centers," between which it is free to rotate. A cord is wrapped around the workpiece and attached at one end to the overhead spring pole and at the other end to the foot treadle on the floor. Pushing down on the treadle spins the workpiece and pulls the spring pole down. This is the cutting stroke. As you let up on the treadle, the action of the spring pole spins the workpiece back in the other direction and readies it for another cutting stroke.

The body of this lathe, and most others, is a bed made from two

The drive rope from the spring pole crosses on the side of the workpiece facing the turner. The right-hand puppet with its conical center is movable along the bed and held in place by a wedge.

Turning tools, from left to right: a skew chisel, two sizes of gouges, and round and diamond-nosed scrapers made from old files.

parallel horizontal timbers. These timbers are mounted on legs that hold them about waist high. The bed provides a track for two upright timbers called "puppets." At least one of these puppets must be movable along the length of the bed and must have some means, such as a wedge or screw arrangement, to allow it to be secured at any point along the bed. The other puppet may be a fixed extension of one of the legs. These puppets, also called the head and tail stocks, have conical, metal centers set into their facing sides. By moving the puppets along the bed, you can adjust the distance between the centers to hold work of different lengths.

The centers are critical pieces of the apparatus. For the lathe to be of any use at all, the two centers must be truly centered pieces themselves: that is, they must be as close as possible to perfect cones. Any roughness or out-of-round places on a center will quickly cause it to enlarge its point of contact with the workpiece, which makes the whole arrangement loose. By far the best "found objects" that I have encountered to use for centers are the points of old industrial weaving shuttles. There are several textile mills upriver from me, so these points turn up now and then, still embedded in bits of the broken dogwood shuttle. Lacking such good fortune, you can use a fixed rest on a grindstone to bring the end of a short length of iron rod to a true, polished cone.

You also need a tool rest that can be fixed at any point on the bed. The top side of the tool rest should be rounded off on the edge away from the rotating work and should be about level with the line between the two centers. The critical thing is to be able to support the turning chisel firmly so that it contacts the work just above the line of the center of rotation.

The driving parts of this lathe are the spring pole, the cord, and the treadle.

The spring pole can be of any lively wood. Up to a point, the longer the pole is, the more even the action. If you are working in cramped quarters, you can use a long spring pole pulling sideways with the cord run over a pulley.

The best cords are made from twisted animal gut or hide. The worst material to use is braided cotton line. A quality hemp rope is a good compromise between these two and is easily obtained. Since it constantly wears against itself as it works, the cord may break occasionally. When it does, the spring pole flies up, hits the ceiling, and knocks the shingles off the roof.

The treadle is a triangular affair that may be either fixed to the floor at its rear end or left free. The diagonal bar must lap on top of the other two pieces or it will fall apart. The cord can be attached at any spot along the length of the long piece to help balance the speed of the lathe with the power needed for a given job. Tying it close to where your foot rests will give you slower speed but greater power; tying it at the far end will give you speed at the cost of power.

Using the Lathe

To use the lathe, first use the drawknife to rough down the stock that you want to turn. Hold it over the bed and give the cord one turn around it so that the cord comes down on the side facing you. Fit the stock between the centers so that it looks right and lightly pinch it up. Try the spin and readjust if necessary

Bring the whole length of the work round before you begin the pattern. Keep the end of the handle well down, the gouge tilted to one side; make a shearing, diagonal cut.

to get it centered. Put a bit of wax or oil on the centers and give the puppets a good squeeze to set the centers. I have no adjustment screw on my spring-pole lathe to keep the centers tight. Instead, I slightly cock the bottom of the movable puppet under the work and then drive the wedge in tight. This forces the centers into the work and keeps them there while I'm working. Adjust the tool rest so that it just clears the work and begin turning.

Turning on the spring-pole lathe is really no different from turning on any other lathe. It takes a little getting used to, but the intermittent action of the lathe quickly becomes natural. If you have never tried one before, you will be pleasantly surprised by just how fast turning on a spring-pole lathe can be.

This chapter is more about lathes than about the art of wood turning itself. However, some basic principles of spindle (long things like chair legs) turning apply to all lathes, no matter how they are powered.

Do as much as possible of the initial rounding of the work by other means before you put it in the lathe. An eccentric workpiece will vibrate as it spins and throw off the accuracy of the points of contact between the wood and the centers.

If you don't have proper turning gouges, you can quickly grind a set of scrapers from old files to get started. The top edge of a scraper does the cutting, so, unlike a gouge, the back end of its handle needs to be held higher than the tool rest so that the cutting edge will contact the work. Turners tend to frown on scrapers, as they require no skill at all to use, but on dry, gnarly wood they may be the only tools that will work.

Start slowly and bring the whole length of the work to a basic cylinder before you begin shaping any of the design. If you have proper turning gouges, use your largest one for this. Hold the back end of the handle well below the top edge of the tool rest. Don't use your gouges as scrapers. Hold the bevel of the gouge so that

Bowl turning is easy and fast on a spring-pole lathe.

it rubs against the spinning work and then rotate the tool so that the cutting edge will make contact. You want to do your cutting with either side of the nose of the gouge, not the point. The object here is to make a shearing cut that you can slide along the length of the work.

When the piece has been brought to a true cylinder, you can pick up speed and begin to cut the pattern that you desire. Make all of your gouge cuts by moving the tool in from the large diameter to the small. In other words, don't try to enlarge a hollow in the work by starting the gouge in the valley and cutting your way back up the sides; it doesn't work. If you think about the relationship of your tool to the spinning work and strive to maintain a diagonal, shearing cut, you can't go far wrong.

Turning a Bowl

One of the more fascinating things that you can do on a lathe is bowl turning. On a spring-pole lathe this calls for a special attachment called a mandrel arm, which spikes into the roughed-out blank of the bowl. This mandrel gives you a place to wrap the drive cord around. The diameter of the mandrel determines the speed of the rotation of the bowl. As in spindle turning, the smaller the diameter of the place where the cord wraps around, the faster the work will spin. I use a 2 1/2-inch-diameter hickory mandrel and usually turn my bowls from half-seasoned sycamore.

Drive the mandrel into the center of the flat side of the bowl blank and set the whole business into the lathe. Turn the outside of the bowl down to size first to get the piece running smoothly. Cutting the inside with a regular, unbent gouge requires the

These four spikes hold the mandrel to the bowl blank. This mandrel is 2 1/2 inches *in diameter. The core left in the bowl is ready to be knocked out and the last bit* *finished by hand.*

removal of a lot of wood before you reach the bottom. When you've done all you can at the lathe, knock off the mandrel, cut out the core, and finish up by hand.

Old-time bowl turners often used curved chisels to turn out a "nest" of a half dozen or more bowls, one inside the other, from a single piece of wood. Sometimes they would fix a stop on the lathe to halt the rotation of the bowl and leave wood for a handle. This stop allowed them only one rotation for each depression of the treadle instead of the eight or so that you get in regular spring-pole bowl work.

Sash Saws

You can also adapt this spring-pole lathe setup into what is essentially a foot-operated, reciprocating band saw. This sort of saw is often called a sash saw because of its similarity to a window sash. The frame fits into the bed of the lathe, where it is fastened in place by wedges driven through the long bottom ends of the uprights. The sash that carries the blade is fastened at its top end to the spring pole and at its bottom end to the foot treadle.

The sawblade (a length of old band-saw blade, if necessary) should have its teeth pointing down so that the cutting is on the down, or power,

stroke. This blade is held in the sash by a bolt that can be turned to adjust the tension of the blade. The tension of the blade holds the mortice and tenon joints of the sash together.

A spring-pole sash saw doesn't have any real advantages over a hand-held turning saw. With one, you hold the work; with the other, you hold the saw.

The Great-Wheel Lathe

The powerful great-wheel lathe was said to run on cheap red wine. The turnwheel could indeed have been someone off the street whom one kept supplied with wine in return for

The spring-pole lathe can be converted to a sash saw, a sort of reciprocating band saw.

Just as in turning, the cutting is done on the downstroke, and the spring pole powers the return.

his labor, or it could have been a family member, apprentice, or grudgingly obliging fellow worker to whom one would have to return the favor. The work of the turnwheel does become easier as the wheel picks up speed, but it is still not a fit use for a human being.

According to tradition, the apprentice serving the wheel stood facing the master turner in order to learn the trade, but I doubt whether he could learn much in that way. The ratio of the diameter of the great wheel to the pulley on the head stock of the lathe usually requires a distance between the two of at least 10 feet. In addition, either the turning tool would have to be on the far side of the lathe or the master turner would have his back to the apprentice. In either case, he might as well look out the window.

The most familiar representations of great-wheel lathes show the wheel in its frame sitting on the floor across

the room from the lathe bed. This is the way I ran mine at first. Inconvenient, and dangerous as well, it took up one whole wall of the shop. Once, when I was walking past it as it was freewheeling, the handle caught on my pants and lifted me half off the floor before ripping itself free. Now, I have the great wheel mounted up in the rafters. This has solved these problems and given me a new advantage—the pull rod allows several people at once to power the lathe for extra-heavy jobs.

I made the outer rim and spokes of my great wheel from a huge white oak that went down in an ice storm. For 132 years that tree had shaded the old churchyard in town. In 1862 someone nailed a poster to the tree—war news, I expect. The four cut nails had been swallowed by the tree and had turned that part of the wood an inky blue. Now, the tree spins around in the rafters of my shop. (It also gets sat upon; it's the

roof over my lumber stack; it's my cabinet workbench.)

The spokes and the rim sections, called fellies, had to be split out and roughed down for two years of drying in the attic. Every few months, I took them down and worked them a little closer to their finished dimensions.

I made the hub from an elm that went down in the same storm. I bored the 1-inch-diameter shaft hole through the rough, dry block and temporarily plugged both ends of this hole with previously turned tapered inserts. The center points on the inserts allowed me to turn the hub true to the axis of the shaft hole.

The times that I spent making the great wheel were some of the best that I can recall. I had excellent wood to work with, and this was my first large wheel. I like to figure things out.

The headstock of my great-wheel lathe came from the wall of an

Mounting the great wheel in the rafters saves a lot of space.

Shaping the inside curve of the white-oak wheel rim sections, or "fellies," with an adz.

The elm hub of the great wheel, 8 inches in diameter. The square end of the shaft holds the driving crank.

The lengths and positions of the spokes are marked with a "speech bat," which mounts on the shaft. The spokes are realigned up and down until the reed on the free end of the bat strikes them all evenly, making the reed vibrate with an even tone.

The six fellies are joined by open mortice and tenon joints and pegs.

The head stock consists of an iron shaft, the apple-wood pulley, and the two bearings of poured "babbit" metal.

abandoned farm building, where it had apparently been belt driven by the same kerosene engine that ran the well pump. Cattle were running free through the buildings of the old homestead. They were apparently enamored of the apple-wood pulley as a scratching post and had polished it to a fine luster. I spent a long day talking to a score of farmers, cousins of farmers, nephews of farmers, and so on, until I finally found the right relative to pay, but I finally got it.

The Treadle Lathe

The treadle lathe is sort of a combination of the spring-pole and the great-wheel lathes: foot power on a treadle turns a crank that turns a wheel that drives the headstock of the lathe. This provides true rotary motion, and one person can do it by himself.

I use this lathe for almost all of my turning, save the very big jobs that need the added power of the great wheel. It's a lot of fun to use and quite efficient: average running speed is 1600 rpm. You are equipped with two motors to run it, so power is never a problem.

The treadle lathe is fast and efficient, and you don't need a helper.

A Reproduction Treadle Lathe

These photographs should enable you to duplicate this lathe if you wish. With this design the entire lathe can be built from standard-dimension softwood lumber. I have shown in the pictures some of the more important features of its construction. There are lots of ways in which this design can be improved upon; think of what bicycles were like a century ago.

This reproduction lathe is made from douglas fir from the lumberyard. The flywheel, idler, and driver pulley all have 1/2-inch-diameter shafts that run in ball bearings set into the frame. The small buttons cover the countersunk wood screws that join the frame together.

The crankshaft is a bent 1/2-inch bolt. It is mounted to the wooden wheel with plumbing flanges and secured with steel pins driven into holes drilled through both the flange and the shaft. These pins must be removed to disassemble the lathe.

The two-foot folding rule leaning against the lower left-hand corner will give you a scale to make your own version if you wish.

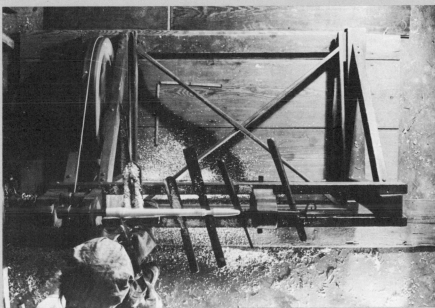

The two-foot rule is lying on the floor in this view. Notice how the diagonal member that supports the front right-hand side of the treadle laps on top of the other one; this forms a sort of cantilever to strengthen the treadle when you work at the right-hand end.

Chapter 11. Blacksmithing

Smithing is an Art-Manual, by which an irregular Lump (or
several Lumps) of Iron, is wrought into an intended Shape.
—Joseph Moxon, *Mechanick Exercises* (1678)

Cutting a length of truck spring to make a drill bit. The bellows are mounted overhead to save floor space.

Knowing how to forge and harden metal is an important step toward self-reliance. Your tools are the language through which you and the wood communicate with one another. The better your understanding of the language, the more use you can make of it. Being able to shape and modify your own tools is the best way to ensure that nothing is missing from your vocabulary.

You don't have to have fancy equipment to get started in iron-working. Think of Humphrey Bogart in *The African Queen*, lap welding a broken propeller shaft over a hearth dug in the ground while Katharine Hepburn pumped the makeshift bellows. Even in real life you can make do with very little. Get the best equipment you can, but don't let anything hold you back.

The main things you need are a forge, a hammer, and an anvil. The forge gives you control over the fire. The fire allows you to soften the metal so that it can be shaped with the hammer on the anvil.

The Forge and the Fire

The primary tool of the metalworker is fire. By blowing air through a charcoal, coke, or coal fire he can heat iron or steel to over 3000° F., so hot that it actually burns up like a Fourth of July sparkler. Control over the air blast is crucial. The first forge that I ever worked with had a fire pot made from an automobile brake drum. The air blast came from an old car-heater blower powered by a twelve-volt battery and controlled by a foot-operated headlight dimmer switch. The dimmer switch offered only two choices, on or off, and the forge had neither damper nor rheostat. Although I burned up and ruined a lot of metal in that forge,

the simple addition of one of these two means of controlling the air flow would have made it entirely satisfactory.

The best thing to look for when beginning blacksmithing is a portable forge with a hand-cranked blower. The way to find one is to ask around. Junk, antique, and scrap dealers see them all the time. All you have to do is find one at a good price. Unless you're like me and buy things half to use and half for the challenge of getting them to work again, don't pay for something until you've figured out how you can fix it. As long as the blower works or can be repaired, you should be able to fix up an air pipe and a fire pot from scrap.

If working at the portable forge gives you the bug, you may want to go all the way and set up a brick forge with a cast-iron fire pot and a double-action bellows. The fire pot is an interesting part of such an arrangement. Many cheap, portable forges have only a perforated grate or grille to separate the air passage from the fuel, along with an arrangement for dumping ashes that fall through the grate. Ashes are not the only problem in forge fires, however; the impurities in coal that are left as the carbon burns off become molten and trickle down to form a lump of nasty sticky slag right over the air inlet. When this slag cools a bit, it turns to hard and glassy clinker. Clinker blocks the air inlet and generally makes the work more difficult. To keep from having to pull the slag up through the fire, smiths invented fire pots incorporating slag-breaking devices. By turning a lever on the side of these fire pots the clinker over the inlet is broken without disturbing the fire. There's no better place for a problem to find ten solutions than in a blacksmith shop.

A cast-iron fire pot. The cylinder in the air inlet rotates on an eccentric arm *controlled from the side of the forge and clears away any clinker buildup that* *blocks the air flow.*

A big, double-action bellows completes the permanent forge setup, not only visually and physically but aurally as well. The ring of the anvil plays a duet with the clacking of the bellows valves. A double-action bellows is so named because it has two chambers: air is forced from a lower chamber into an upper chamber that acts as a reservoir. This keeps the flow of air steady and even rather than the puff-puff of a fireplace bellows.

I had been looking for an old bellows for some years before I finally bought one at an auction. The century-old leather on it was completely rotten and covered with dozens of pathetic patches. The story

behind the patches began to unfold when I disassembled the bellows. Once I finally had the old leather off the sides, I could see that at one time a mouse had crawled up the air pipe from the forge and, unable to find his way out the way he came in, gnawed an exit hole around the side of the internal valve. Upon finding himself in the lower chamber and still not out, he apparently chewed through the leather and went off looking for a better home. The smith was able to patch the mouse hole in the leather, but the damage to the internal valve was not so easy to fix. I could see where he had reached up through the lower valve hole in an attempt to patch the internal valve with calico,

glue, and wood. This effort was only partially successful, however. The internal valve still leaked so badly that when the lower chamber was taking in air, it also drew air from the fire back into the upper chamber. The live sparks that came with this air burned through the leather sides. This was the reason for all the small patches; you could read in the stitches the futility of his efforts. This would have happened about the time that the automobile was displacing the horse, and with the shoeing trade on the decline, I guess the old man just gave up.

This old anvil weighs 119 pounds, as indicated by the number 107 marked on the side in old-style measurement. The first number is in hundredweights, or 112 pounds. The second number is in *quarter hundredweights, or 28 pounds. The third number is additional pounds. This anvil weighs 1 hundredweight, 0 quarter hundredweights, and 7 additional pounds. On the hardened face of* *the anvil are a ball-peen hammer, a cross-peen hammer, and a hardie sitting in the square hardie hole. The pritchel or punch hole is just visible behind the hardie.*

Hammers

Although in Britain the ball-peen hammer seems to be more widely used, most American smiths prefer a hammer with a cross peen. The shapes of the two hammers affect metal in different ways. Hitting the hot iron with the ball on the ball peen or with the slightly crowned flat of either hammer causes the metal to spread in all directions; the cross peen, however, will spread it pri- marily in two directions only. The advantage of the cross peen is evident when you want to stretch something out longer without mak- ing it any wider. In any case, most of the work is done with the face of the hammer, not the peen. A forging hammer can weigh from two to three pounds for your own hammer, and from five to twenty pounds for the sledge wielded by an assistant, or "striker," who follows the smith's lead, blow for blow.

Anvils

A lively anvil is the one of the greatest assets a smith can possess. It may be hard to think of a two- hundred-pound block of iron and steel as being lively, but the re- siliency of the hardened steel face makes a great difference in the efficiency of the work. The rebound of the hammer from a good anvil, as opposed to the energy drain of a dead anvil, can mean the difference

The leg vise transfers shock and torque directly to the floor. Two sledge hammers are visible behind the vise. The quench tub in the foreground holds water to control the fire and cool the iron.

between hard work and miserable work.

The bodies of quality anvils are wrought iron or steel, forged with massive hammer blows into their familiar shape. This shape, known as the "London pattern," has evolved over the centuries as the most useful configuration for general work. The hardened face is, of course, where most of the work gets done. At one end this face drops off to a soft table that is not hardened. This soft table is used as a work surface when cutting with a chisel to prevent damage to the tool or the anvil face. It is better, however, to use a plate of soft steel set aside especially for such cutting; there's no need to mess up the anvil by using it as a chopping block. Beyond the soft table is the bick or horn of the anvil. The round surface of the horn supports bends and curves as they are hammered. It can also act in much the same way as the cross-peen hammer in directing the spreading force of the hammer blows. At the other end of the anvil are two holes through the hanging end of the face. The square "hardie" hole provides a socket for accessory tools, such as the upright cut-off chisel, or hardie, itself. The smaller, round hole, or pritchel, is used to support metal being pierced with hammer-driven punches and drifts.

Mount the anvil securely on a wooden block. The face of the anvil should just touch your knuckles as you stand alongside it. An elm stump is the traditional wood for this job, not because it does the job better than other species, but because it's too tough to split up for firewood.

I have worked on various scrap-yard substitutes for proper anvils with varying degrees of success. Any sufficiently massive block of iron or steel will get you started. Anvils are generally sold by the pound; useful sizes range from seventy-five to three hundred pounds, but look for quality rather than weight. A good anvil has a clear bell-like tone when struck and will bounce a hammer back like a golf ball dropped on the sidewalk.

Leg Vises

If you are considering spending money for a metalworking vise, I advise you to hold off buying a bench or machinist's vise and try instead to locate a good leg vise. Although the leg vise is also mounted on the surface of the bench, the steel leg extending down to the floor makes all the difference. This leg transmits shock directly to the floor and steadies the vise so well against tipping that its uses are limited more by your strength than by its own.

Chisels

Chisels can be classed as either cold or hot chisels, depending on the temperature of the metal they are intended to cut. They differ in hardness and shape. Cold chisels are quite hard and have a short, thick taper to cut cold metal; hot chisels are used to cut softer, hot metal and have a long, slender taper. Chisels may also have a handle attached so that they may be struck with the sledge, which qualifies them as "set" chisels, or they may have a shaft to fit into the square anvil hole, which makes them hardies.

Punches

Punches may be held either directly or by an attached handle. The business end is squared off, not

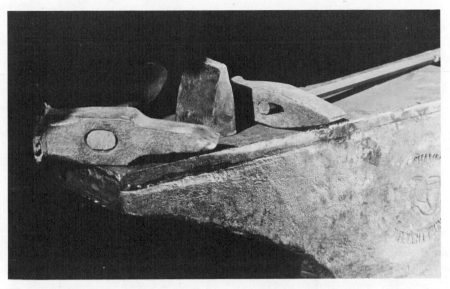

A narrow-necked hot chisel, a hardie, and a cold chisel sit on the hardened steel face of this wrought-iron anvil. Iron-working tools with handles are often called "set" tools; thus we have a hot set, a hardie, and a cold set.

pointed, and removes a slug of metal. You can enlarge holes made with the punch by hammering tapered "drifts" through them.

Tongs, Fullers, Swedges, and Flatters

Beyond saying what they are, there is not enough space here to cover the wide variety of tools used by practicing smiths. Tongs, of course, hold a workpiece that is too hot to handle. I suggest you buy a few and copy them to make you own later on. Fullers resemble rounded chisels or the cross peen of the hammer and can be hand-held "top" fullers or square-shanked "bottom" fullers that fit into the hardie hole. Swedges, like fullers, come in top and bottom models, but are concave and form a die between which the hot iron is molded. Flatters are flat faced tools that are struck with the sledge to finish off a hammered surface. All

these tools will come to you when you need them.

The Fire

Although charcoal and coke are often used as fuel, bituminous coal is the smith's major source of heat. Check with local coal dealers to see what other smiths in the area have been using. Ideally, you should use sulfur-free coal that is about the size of small marbles and about one-fourth coal dust by weight.

Water is an essential part of a coal fire. Soak the coal down with water and pack it around the air inlet, leaving a place for the kindling to go. Stuff some balled-up paper and shavings down in the hole, light it, and let it get burning well before you start pumping much air through. When the kindling is going well, place some coal on top of it and give the fire enough air to get this new coal going as well. As the coal begins to burn, the volatile impurities will cause foul smoke. These impurities can damage the metal being heated. Once these are driven off, however, the fire begins to form coke, which burns clean and hot. Coke is constantly being formed around the perimeter of the fire; it is the stuff that you want to have burning, not green coal. For this reason you should feed the fire as you work by knocking in coke from the sides of the fire, rather than drop in fresh coal from the top. Use water to keep the fire confined to where you want it and use no more air than you need.

When you heat metal in the fire, always keep sufficient fuel beneath the iron. If you let the fire burn "hollow" beneath the iron, it may heat the iron sufficiently, but the free oxygen in the air blowing on the metal will quickly oxidize it, forming scale or causing it to burn up completely. A deep fire will consume most of the oxygen before it reaches the metal. You don't want the iron to lie entirely on top of the fire either, for the free air will cause the same problem. Keep the iron covered in glowing coke.

Iron and Steel

Wrought iron is the traditional metal of the smith's trade. The combination of low-carbon iron and slag from the manufacturing process gives it a fibrous quality. Like wood, wrought iron has a distinct grain, which can be plainly seen in weathered work made from this material. It can be worked over a wide range of heats; moreover, it welds easily and has other characteristics that make it desirable for hand forging.

Wrought iron is no longer generally available, having been supplanted by a metal known as mild

steel. Mild steel is pure iron with a higher percentage of carbon than wrought iron. It is still basically iron and has a homogenous or granular, rather than fibrous, texture. Mild steel will not hold an edge and cannot be adequately hardened by heat treatment.

When steel is combined with enough carbon, around 1 percent, it can be hardened by heat treatment to hold a cutting edge. This is high-carbon steel, the material of the edge tools of the woodworker.

All of these forms of iron (including cast iron, which you can't do much with) can be found in scrap yards. Old buggy and wagon parts are a good source for wrought iron. Truck springs are usually the right kind of high-carbon steel for forging cutting tools, and mild steel for general work is everywhere. Scrap yards are also good places to look for tools, leg vises, and everything else. You buy it by the pound.

Processes

As the old chestnut goes, black-smithing is essentially getting the right metal, heating it to the right heat, and hitting it in the right place. The processes involved are, briefly, bending, drawing out (making it thinner), upsetting (making it thicker), punching, cutting, welding, and heat treating (controlling hardness). The following projects—the spike dog, the cant hook, the froe, and retempering a chisel—will serve as a good introduction to all of these techniques.

A Spike Dog

Spike dogs are giant staples that hold logs steady while they are worked on. The two chisellike points of the dog are at right angles to one another to match the grain of the support log

The spike dog is a giant staple.

and the log being hewn or sawed. Forging spike dogs involves cutting to length, bending the angles, squaring or "upsetting" the angles, and drawing out the points.

Cut a 20-inch or so length of 1/2-to-3/4-inch square or round mild steel. The metal may be cut hot by bringing it to yellow heat and cutting all the way around on the hardie or with a hot chisel. When cutting on the hardie, be sure to make the final blow a shearing cut to the side of the hardie to avoid damaging it with the hammer.

Next, heat the bar to a bright yellow, centering on a point about 3 inches from the end. Bend the bar at this point by clamping it in the vise and pulling or hammering it over the edge of the anvil. Do not try to tighten up the radius of the curve; keep it somewhat gentle.

With the bend still at or reheated to a bright yellow, cool the last 2 inches of the bent end by sticking it in the water of the quench tub until it just stops glowing. This will localize the heat in the bend area where you want it. Hold the opposite end of the bar and slam the cooled end down on the face of the anvil with repeated blows. This will start to thicken, or upset, the hot metal in the corner to enable you to fill out the right angle. Reheat if necessary and start slamming down with the bar held vertically. Keep an eye on the inside radius of the bend; you don't want it to fold up. Continue this process until you see that you can finish refining the square corner with the hammer.

To draw out the point, bring the last 2 inches of the bent bar to a yellow heat. Draw the taper out by hammering over the horn of the anvil or by striking it with the cross peen on the face of the anvil. Smooth out the taper by holding it flat on the anvil and striking with the

Cut the bar for the spike dog to length by tumbling it on the hardie as you strike down with the hammer.

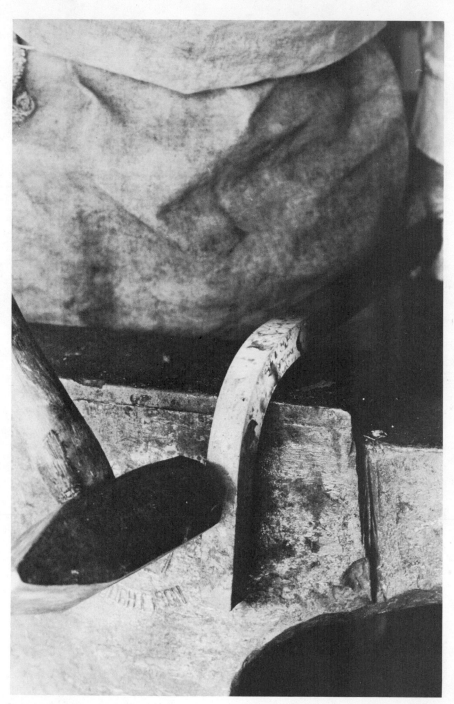

Bend the bar in a gentle right angle.

face of the hammer. Turn the piece 90° every so often and hammer back any side spread.

Repeat these steps on the other end with the point at 90° to this first one.

A Cant Hook

The cant hook is another tool for handling heavy logs. The iron swing hook grabs the log and allows it to be turned or rolled with the leverage of the long wooden arm. Forging the hook involves upsetting, drawing out, punching the pivot hole, and bending.

Cut a 14-inch length of mild steel that measures 7/8 inch by 1/2 inch, or as close to this as you can muster. For ease in handling, you can leave the bar twice as long as necessary and cut it only when you have to. Bring the last inch of one end to a bright yellow heat and upset (thicken) it by slamming the bar down vertically on the anvil. If the end of the bar is not square or if you don't hit straight down with it, you may get bending to the sides. Bring it back in line with the hammer before it goes too far.

With the upset end still at yellow heat, hold the bar on edge on the face of the anvil so that the thickened end hangs over the far end. Hammer down on the overhanging end a few blows, pull the end of the bar back on the face, turn it so it lies flat, and strike it to compensate for sideways spread. Alternate hammering the bar in these two positions to bring the thickened metal around to the side; then draw this out to a point at right angles to the length of the bar.

Upset the last inch of the opposite end of the bar in the same way as before; then hammer this bulge flat until the bar is the same thickness as before, but wider. This strengthens

Hold the bar at the far end and slam the bend down on the face of the anvil to begin to force the metal into a corner. Then slam the bend down on the anvil with the long end of the bar held straight up and down.

Finally, slam down with the short end down. Alternate between these three positions until the bend is brought into a right angle.

Refine the right angle and correct any sideways spread with the hammer.

Draw out the point with the cross peen.

the area to be punched. Bring this end to a yellow heat, set it on the flat of the anvil, and drive in a 1/2-inch punch until it is about three-fourths the way through. Don't try to go all the way through, but quickly flip the bar, set it over the pritchel hole, center the punch on the bulge, and drive it on through, knocking out a slug of metal. Smooth up the inside of the hole by rocking the punch around in a circular motion.

To bend the bar bring as much of the length as possible to an orange yellow heat, set it on the horn of the anvil, and hammer bend it by striking on the far side of where it makes contact. Keep the bar from thickening or mushrooming by intermittently hammering it flat on the face of the anvil. The bar needs a sharper bend near the point than at the eye end.

To complete the cant hook, set it in a mortice cut through an oak, hickory, or ash handle about 2 inches in diameter and about 36 inches long. When fully closed, the end of the hook should lie on the end of the handle. Pin through the pivot hole in the hook with a 1/2-inch carriage bolt and peen over the threads to keep the nut from falling off.

A Froe

As you have seen, froes are valuable tools. They are exceedingly simple things in themselves, but not terribly easy to make. The process of forge welding the eye shut can be explained very quickly, but will take a considerable time to master.

Select a piece of mild steel about 3/8 inch thick, 2 inches wide, and 18 inches long. Of this length, 8 inches will be taken up in making the eye, leaving a 10-inch-long blade. Bring one end of the bar to a bright yellow

The cant hook.

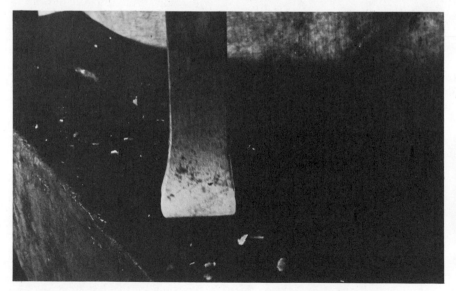

To begin shaping the hook, upset (thicken) the end of the bar by slamming it straight down on the anvil face.

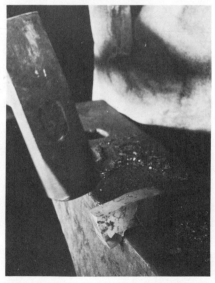

Force the thickened end to one side by hammering it over the edge of the anvil. Prevent any sideways spread by hammering it flat on the anvil face.

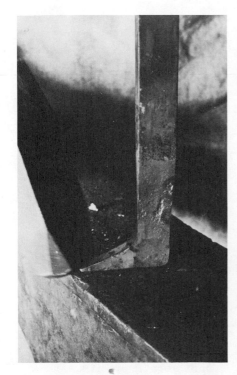

Draw the hook to a point by hammering on the anvil face.

Drive the punch three-fourths of the way through the end. Do this on the flat of the anvil, not over the pritchel hole.

Flip the bar over, set it over the pritchel hole, and drive the punch through. The punch will pop out a slug and leave both sides flat.

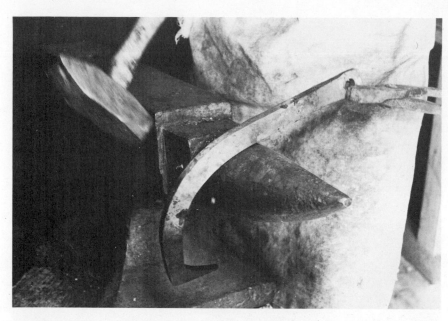

Bend the bar into the curve by hanging it over the horn of the anvil and hammering on the far side.

The welded eye of the froe is the hard part.

heat and draw down the last 1 1/2 inches or so with an even taper. Leave this taper slightly crowned on one face. This is the area that will be welded back to the blade after the eye is formed. This thinning will make the welded area even; the crowning will cause the middle of this area to make contact first and cause any debris that would interfere with the weld to be forced out the sides when the two pieces are hammered together. This preparation is called "scarfing."

Bring the last 8 inches of the scarfed end to a bright yellow heat and bend it over at a gentle right angle where the eye will begin. Be sure to bend the right way so that the scarf will be in the correct place when the eye is closed. Hammer this bent length over the horn of the anvil to bring the eye back around. When you have almost closed the eye, place a 1 1/2-inch-diameter mandrel (a length of pipe or scrap truck axle will do) in the eye to support it as you squeeze the ends shut in the vise. Pull the mandrel out and get ready to weld.

Forge welding literally makes one piece of metal out of two. Not only must the two surfaces be hot enough to fuse together, but there must not be anything in between them. The oxide that forms on heated iron or steel can prevent a successful weld. To prevent this oxide from forming, a flux of borax or fine sand is placed on the two surfaces. This melts and forms a coating like melted glass, which protects the metal from the air. The flux also combines with any oxide that is already present and lowers its melting point so that it can be squeezed out to the sides when the scarfed joint is hammered shut.

Set the prepared joint in a deep, clean fire. Make sure that it is covered in hot coke, but don't let

Prepare the end to be welded by hammering it into a tapered, convex scarf.

Start the loop of the eye by bending it to a gentle right angle.

Bring the loop back around by hammering it over the horn of the anvil.

Close up the eye by placing a length of pipe in the opening and squeezing the overlap in the vise.

Bring the eye to a white heat; it should just begin to spark. Bring it instantly to the anvil and hammer the joint shut.

any crud get in between the two pieces. When the joint is red hot, put enough flux on the two surfaces to cover them. Slowly bring up the heat until the metal just starts to spark and then quickly bring it to the anvil and hammer it shut. Hit the middle first to send flux flying in all directions and then move out to the sides to close them up. Speed is critical here. Continue striking as the heat dies down to help refine the grain structure of the metal. The nature of the iron or steel that you are working with will have a lot to do with the success of the weld. If it doesn't work, try some other stock or use a lower or higher heat. The lower the carbon content of the metal, the higher the heat it can take and the easier forge welding will be.

If your first attempts at forge welding prove unsuccessful, don't be too discouraged. You can still live with a froe that has an unwelded (we'll call it a "French") eye. About one out of every ten old froes that I have seen have had faulty welds held shut with rivets. So, with eye welded tight or not, begin to draw one edge of the blade to a blunt splitting angle. Heat the blade bright yellow hot and bend it by hammering it over the horn so that it is slightly convex on the opposite side of the blade from the edge to be tapered. This will compensate for the tendency of the blade to bend in the opposite direction as it is drawn out; the two forces will cancel each other out when you're done. Draw the edge to a blunt taper with the cross-peen hammer on the face of the anvil. Finish up by hitting with the flat of the hammer. Avoid hitting the face of the anvil with the corner of the hammer by holding the bevel of the blade on the far edge of the face.

A walnut tree

A walnut chair

A white-oak chair

A white-oak tree

Draw out the splitting edge to a blunt chisel point.

Tempering a Chisel

Whether you forge your own tools or buy them, the ability to control the hardness of steel tools is an invaluable skill. I knew a fellow once who used to burn the broken handle out of an axe head by throwing it in the wood stove. When he cleaned out the ashes, he would retrieve it and put a new handle in. Later, he would wonder why it wouldn't hold an edge. Of course, he had inadvertently annealed the axe so that it became soft. The fire had heated the high-carbon steel of the axe head beyond a critical point (red or yellow

hot). Then the slow cooling had allowed the crystalline structure to reform in the softest arrangement. If, however, he had taken the axe head out of the fire at the critical temperature and cooled it rapidly in water, he would have made the head so hard and brittle that he could have shattered it like glass. Taking this process one step further, if he had released some of this brittleness by reheating the fully hardened head until just the desired amount of hardness was left, he would have had a good axe again. This is called "tempering."

An easy way to harden and temper something like a chisel or gouge uses residual heat from the harden-

ing process to temper the edge. This technique is called "point tempering."

Heat the last 2 or 3 inches of a chisel to a dark yellow heat in the forge. Build up to this heat slowly enough that it heats all the way through, not just on the surface. Once it arrives at the right heat, harden the end by sticking the last inch in a tub of room-temperature water. Keep it moving around and slightly up and down so that there will not be a sharp temperature differential at any one point, which could cause a crack. As soon as the inch of metal in the water has lost all its glow, pull the chisel out of the

*This corner chisel was pulled from the ashes of a house fire and will not hold an edge.
To reharden it, it must first be brought to a yellow heat.*

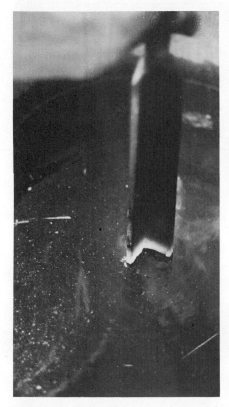

*Quench the last inch in room-
temperature water until the glow in the
submerged area disappears. Keep it moving slightly up and down as you do this.*

*As soon as the glow is gone, pull it from the water and polish the surface with an
abrasive stone. Work fast. Watch the temper colors move into the cooled area.*

water and quickly polish the oxide off of the cutting edge with an abrasive stone so that you can see the bright metal. Watch this surface, because soon the residual heat from the unquenched body of the chisel will flow down into the quenched, hardened point. This heat will effect the tempering of the cutting edge and will be accompanied by the appearance of oxidation colors on the polished surface. The key to tempering is to look for the color that indicates the degree of temperature that you desire and then stop the process at that point by plunging the whole tool into the water. The first color to appear will be a faint yellow, which gradually turns to a deeper straw (I stop here for chisels and adzes). This is followed by a bronze, which turns brown, spotted with purple, then a full purple (axes), and then on down to blue. Remember that the progression of colors means increasing heat and an increasingly softer edge. Act quickly when the color you want arrives, but if you see the parade of colors down to the edge slowing down so that it looks like the right one is going to stop right where you want it, so much the better. A long, slow parade is better for the tool than a short, fast one. Remember also that you can get these colors to appear on any iron or steel but only high-carbon steel can be hardened and tempered like this.

It takes a lifetime to learn the skills of tempering and metalworking in general. The brief instructions here have been largely schematic; many pitfalls and shortcuts have been left unmarked. There are, however, excellent resources available. If you are interested in pursuing metal-working further, you should have little trouble finding more detailed guides.

When the right color reaches the edge, quench the whole tool by plunging it up and down in the water tub.

Chapter 12. Dovetails

The unities, Sir . . . are a completeness—a kind of universal dove-tailedness with regard to place and time.
—Charles Dickens, *Nicholas Nickleby* (1838)

Dovetail joints connect the ends of boards together somewhat like interlocking the fingers of two hands. The difference is that fingers are alike on both hands. They can go together right into left, or left into right. It doesn't matter from what angle they are put together or pulled apart. In contrast, dovetail joints will go together or come apart in one direction only. The wedge-shaped dovetails on the end of one board fit into the spaces between the pins on the end of the other board. These two boards can be separated only by pulling the dovetails straight out the same way that they went in.

When you make a dovetailed box, first decide which direction you want this freedom of movement to lie in. Most boxes are rectangular, with distinctly shorter ends and longer sides. The tail and pin arrangement should depend on what the box will be used for and in what direction most of the internal pressure will be exerted—to the sides or out the ends. The boards with the pins cut in them have a much greater resistance to being pushed or pulled apart from the box than do the boards with the tails. That is why a dovetailed drawer always has the pins cut into the board that has the handles on it. In a long, narrow chest stuffed with blankets most of the internal pressure pushes against the front and back boards. Accordingly, these should be the ones to receive the pins. If there are carrying handles on the ends of the box, then the ends should get the pins. In chests and boxes, however, the aesthetic considerations of showing off the dovetails on the most visible side may override the mechanical aspects of the design.

Before you begin dovetailing the box, you must also decide how large to cut the tails relative to the pins. In general, the narrower the pins, the finer the work is considered.

However, dovetails cut to the standards and needs of a carpenter would look out of place on a piece of fine cabinetry; while a cabinetmaker's fine, narrow joints would look strange on a carpentry job. When deciding on the size of your dovetails, try for the right balance between aesthetics and function.

A final question is which to cut first, the tails or the pins. This question is as old as the question about the chicken and the egg and about as important. Both sides have their champions, but one consideration is that you can clamp together all the boards needing dovetails and saw them at the same time. You can't do this with the pins because of the way they are shaped. Since one of the two elements of the joint has to be custom fitted to the other, the time saved by gang cutting the tails usually decides the issue.

I find that most of the dovetailing that I do in my business is for making quick and inexpensive boxes and chests. On these I use the basic "open dovetail," a joint that leaves the tails and pins plainly visible from both the front and side. Working fast, I make the pins first, cutting them by eye with no layout. The approach is similar to that which was used to get the legs of the shaving horse evenly splayed. I make my first cut and then use it to judge the rest.

Dovetailing a Box

The first step in making a box is to see that all four boards are cut square and true, and are equal in thickness and width. Set a marking gauge or some other similar contrivance, such as a combination square, to the

Scribe all the way around the ends of all boards.

Softer wood may need more splay to compensate for its lower compressive strength. A bevel setting of 1:5 is about as wide as you can safely get. Harder woods will hold with as low an angle as 1:8. A setting of 1:7 is a good average.

thickness of the boards, plus a hair. With this setting, scribe all the way around the ends of all the boards with the fence of the gauge held against the end grain. This delineates the length of the tails and pins. The "plus a hair" will leave small protrusions on the tails and pins that can be planed off after the joint is assembled. If you are joining boards of unequal thickness, use the thickness of one of the boards of one size to set the gauge for scribing the boards of the other size.

Clamp the piece that will have the pins on it upright in a bench vise or kneel on it with the side that will become the outside of the box facing away from you. Before you start sawing, get a clear mental picture of what you are about to do. When you're cutting pins, essentially what you're doing is making spaces to put the dovetails into. When you make, say, three spaces for three dovetails, you're left with two half pins on either end of the board and two full pins in between. The angles of these spaces across the end grain of the pin board determine the divergent angles of the spread on the dovetails. Too sharp a spread will weaken the dovetails; too little spread will cost you holding power. Hardwoods with a greater long-grain shear resistance could take a sharper spread than softwoods. The photo shows how you can determine safe angles by setting a bevel gauge on a framing square. When you have set the proper angle on the gauge, you can use it to lay out the pattern for pins or tails each time you cut them, or you can commit it to memory and work by eye.

Making the pins (or spaces) for three dovetails calls for six saw cuts:

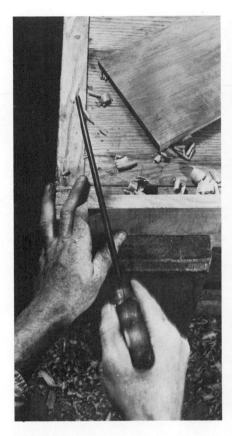

Cut 1.

Cut 2.

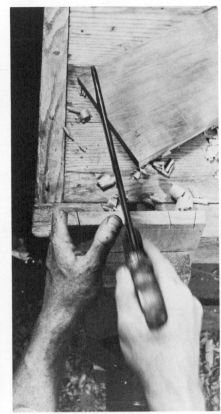

Cut 4.

CUT 1. Set the saw (the finest one you have) on the left-hand side of the board at what you judge to be the proper angle and the proper distance from the end. Saw straight down until you just barely touch the line that was scribed with the marking gauge.

CUT 2. Move over to the right-hand side of the board and make a second cut just like the first except angled the other way.

CUT 3. This cut, along with cut 2, defines the dimensions of the right-hand tail space. Make it the desired distance to the left and parallel to 1.

CUT 4. Exactly halfway between cut 1 and cut 3 and parallel to them both.

CUT 5. Parallel to cut 2, this cut, along with cut 1, determines the dimensions of the left-hand tail space.

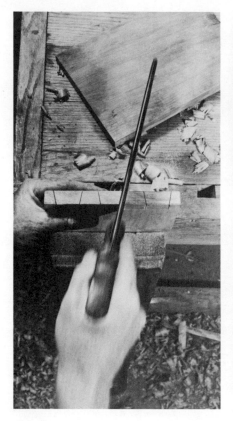

Cut 6.

Cut out the waste with a coping saw.

CUT 6. Halfway between and parallel to cut 2 and cut 5.

These six saw cuts have prepared the way for making the spaces for three dovetails. The process for cutting the pins for a greater number of dovetails by eye is pretty much the same. It is, however, easier visually to divide a space in half than into thirds. This is why I aim for three, five, or nine tails and try to avoid four or seven.

Clearing Out

Think, now, and mark the wood that is to be removed. I usually work in softwoods and cut out the waste blocks with a coping saw. In hardwoods, cutting in from both sides with bevelsided bench chisels may give you better results. However you do it, you should be sure not to cut below the line scribed with the marking gauge on both sides of the board. Remember that you have been facing the side of the board that will be to the interior of the box. You want to cut just to the scribed line on both sides, but it is the outside that will be seen.

Cutting the Tails

The tails are cut to match the pins exactly. Set the board with the already cut pins on the scribed edge of the interior side of the board that is to have the tails cut in it. Line it up just right so that the inside edges of the pins are exactly on the scribed line of the board. Using a knife or fine scribe, mark the insides of the tail spaces onto the board.

Mount this board upright in the vise with the scribed lines facing you. Use a square to draw these lines back across the end grain. Mark the pieces that will be cut away. This is critical, for you must now be sure to cut only on the *waste* side of the line. This is what gives you a tight joint. Make all of your down cuts exactly square and just barely touching the scribed line.

Be careful not to go below the line.

Clean up with a paring chisel.

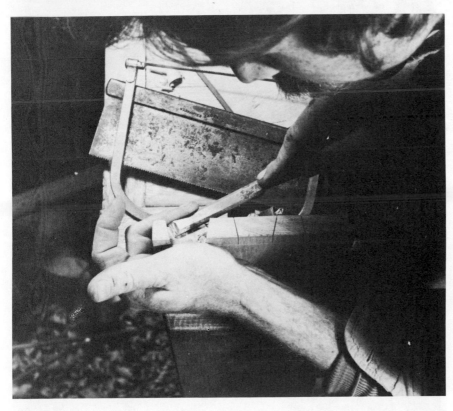

Set the board with the pins on the board that will have the tails and carefully scribe the spaces to be cut.

Be absolutely sure to cut on the waste side of the scribed line.

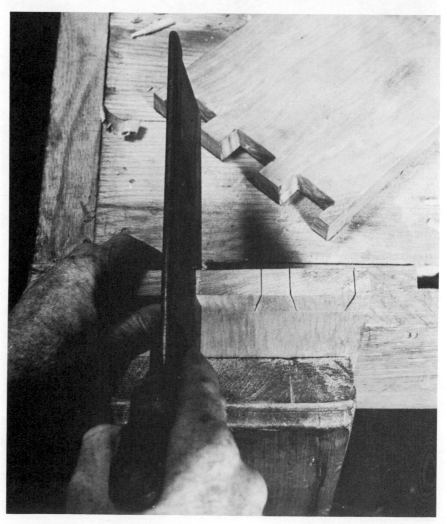

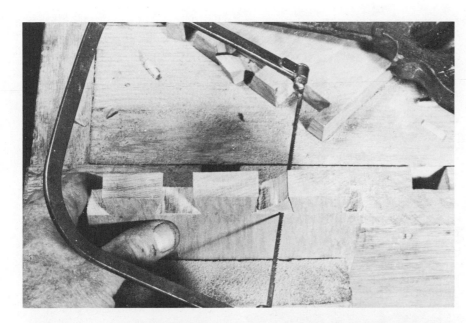

Remove the waste pieces with the coping saw and clean up with a chisel.

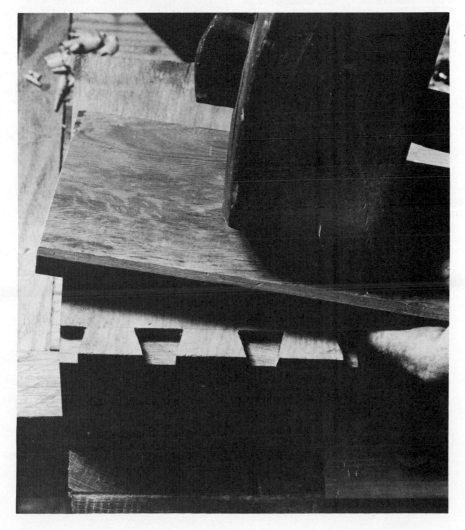

Drive the two pieces together; too tight a fit can split the pin board.

Half-blind dovetails won't show on the front of this old drawer.

Scribe the length of the dovetails on the end grain of the drawer front and around the ends of the two drawer sides while they are clamped together in a vise. Here the groove for the drawer bottom has already been plowed in all pieces.

Cut out the waste blocks with the coping saw and clean up any surplus with a razor-sharp chisel.

Check the two boards for fit. No one does it their first time, but dovetail joints are meant to be put together only once. If you try them out several times before you glue them (if you glue them), the wood will be compressed and won't give as tight a joint. It's best to apply the glue first and join them together only once. During assembly be especially careful that the two outside dovetails aren't such a tight fit that you split the pin board.

Half-Blind Dovetails

Drawers are usually put together with half-blind dovetails, which leave the front of the drawer with no joint showing. The main stress on a drawer is the repeated pulling on the front board when it is opened. Obviously, this is not where you

want that one direction of weakness to lie. Thus, the pins are always cut in the drawer front and the tails in the sides.

For this job you should cut the tails first. Set the marking gauge to the depth that you want the tails to protrude into the drawer front and scribe with this setting on the end grain of the front board, gauging from the back side. With the same setting, scribe around the ends of the side boards where the tails will be cut. Reset the scribe to the thickness of the side boards and scribe down the inside of the drawer front to mark the depth of the pins.

Lay out the dovetails in the side boards. If you wish, use a pair of dividers to get them all spaced evenly. You can, as I said earlier, cut them all at once by clamping them together in the vise.

Take a prepared side board and align it precisely on the drawer front where it will go. Scribe the outline of the tails onto the end grain of the front. With a square, transfer the ends of these lines straight down the inside of the front to the line scribed with the gauge. Mark the spaces to be cut away.

Set the drawer front straight up in the vise with the inside facing you. Again on the waste side of the line, cut down on an angle as much as you can with your finest saw. From here on, it's all done with chisels.

I know everyone will be impressed with your dovetails, just as you should be. Half-blind dovetailing is a major watershed in woodworking. You're now peering down into the valley of the cabinetmakers.

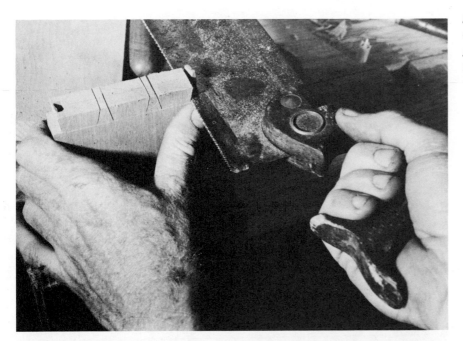

*Saw the dovetails on the drawer sides
while they are clamped together. The
groove for the bottom must be contained in
the end dovetail or it will show as a gap.*

*Cut out the waste with a coping saw and
clean up with a chisel.*

Scribe the outline of the dovetails onto the drawer front.

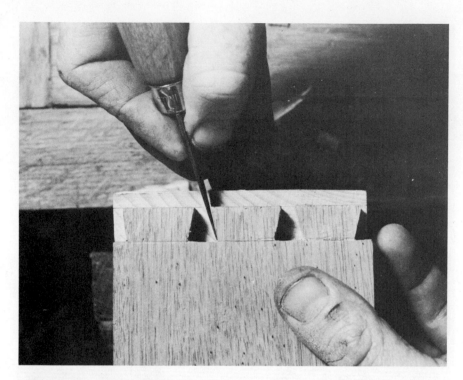

Make angled saw cuts to start the pins.

Finish up by chopping down with a chisel.

The groove for the drawer bottom is completely hidden when the joint is driven together.

Chapter 13. Panel-Frame Construction

A clavestock, and rabbetstock, carpenters crave,
and seasoned timber, for pinwood to have.
—Thomas Tusser, *Five Hundred Points of Husbandry* (1557)

The panels in the cabinet door must be free to move within the frame. The two outer vertical pieces are stiles, the middle piece is a mullion, and the top and bottom pieces are the rails.

A good door—one that fits tightly in its frame, impervious both to cold drafts and to pests—is something we too often take for granted. I did myself until I lived for several years in a tepee with a canvas door. My Toggenberg goats, which preferred my books and clothes to anything they could find outside to eat, were a constant reminder of the importance of a secure door. Wooden doors have long been a feature of house and furniture construction. Their development represented sophisticated advancements in the understanding of the properties of the materials involved.

The problem was that wood is a dynamic material. It expands when it takes on moisture and shrinks when it dries out. To be effective, a door must remain the same size. It shouldn't swell up and stick in the summer or shrink and open up cracks in the winter. Obviously, a door that incorporates a solid expanse of wood is always affected by changes in the weather. The solution was to design a door that allowed the inevitable movement of the wood to take place within a stable framework.

Wood swells and shrinks considerably across the grain and hardly at all along it. The wider a board is, the greater is its potential for shrinking and swelling. A door frame made of relatively narrow boards will have little tendency to change its dimensions. Grooves cut all the way around on the inside faces of this frame will create spaces within which wider boards can float and move as they wish. The wide boards can expand further into the grooves as they swell in the summer without pushing the frame out. In the dryer winter the wide boards shrink, but

they still remain within the grooves
and don't create openings. This is
panel-frame construction.

The Frame

Vertical pieces, or stiles, and horizontal pieces, or rails, make up the
frame. An intermediate stile is called
a mullion. The pieces of the frame
are joined to one another with
mortice and tenon joints. Usually the
stiles are full length from top to
bottom, and the rails are set between
these. This puts the tenons on the
rails and the mortices in the stiles.

  The panel-frame door that I'm
shown making here was for my work
bench. The frame was made from
some white-oak boards from an old
pig sty, which accounts for some of
the tenons being shorter than I
would normally want them. The
ammonia treatment from years of pig
urine turned the oak a beautiful grey-
brown, so I used it in spite of
occasionally having to cut things
a bit short.

Squaring Up the Stock

First, bring all of the pieces to size.
Choose the best face side on each
piece and plane it perfectly flat and
true. Next plane one of the narrow
sides, checking the right angle with a
try square. Set a marking gauge for
the width you want the board to be
and, riding against the side that you
planed last, scribe the width of the
stile or rail down both sides. Plane it
down to this width and check it with
the try square. Now set the gauge for
the thickness that you want the
frame boards to be and scribe this
down both edges, riding against the
face that you planed first. Plane

*Plane one face perfectly true and use it to gauge the rest of the dimensions of the
frame pieces.*

Plane down to the lines scribed with the gauge. This makes the opposite faces of the stock parallel.

down this back side to the lines and then recheck the whole thing. To avoid having to reset the gauge do each of these steps to all the pieces at the same time.

Plowing the Groove

The groove that holds the panel should be the same width as the thickness of the tenons that hold the frame together. By the old rule, this dimension should be less than half but more than a third of the thickness of the wood. A plow plane is the right tool for making this sort of groove. The adjustable fence and interchangeable irons allow you to meet the needs of different-sized frames. A simple grooving plane will also do the job if it is the right size. If you're determined, and have nothing else, you can do the whole job with a chisel.

You will also need a morticing chisel of the same width as the plow-plane iron to cut out the mortices. Before you do any plowing or

morticing, lay out the lines where they will go. Set a marking gauge to scratch out the width of the chisel down the center of the inside edge of the frame. If you have only a single-pointed gauge rather than a double-pointed morticing gauge, you will have to do this with two settings. Always gauge against the face side of all pieces. When marking the rails and the mullion, go all the way around the end, as this will be your guide when cutting the tenons.

Plow all the grooves on all the pieces. Do this before you start morticing because the groove cuts away part of the width of the tenons. A common beginner's mistake is to cut the mortices to the width of the ungrooved rails, resulting in mortices that are too long. Start planing at the far end and work your way back. The wider the panel, the deeper the groove should be.

Tenoning

The tenon shoulders must be perfectly square if the joint is going to look good and work well. Hold a square up tight against the side of the rail and draw a knife across the face to cut the line of the shoulder down into the wood. Come back down this line with the chisel tilted to the waste side of the line to form a long slot to start the saw in. Carry the shoulder line of the tenon around to the back side with the square and slice a groove there. Using your best saw, cut these shoulders down to the lines scribed on the side with the marking gauge. I always split off the excess wood on the cheeks of the tenon if the grain looks true. Some people always saw them. Using one of these methods, get rid of this wood and then flatten and smooth the cheeks by shaving across the grain with a plane or chisel held flat on the wood with the bevel up.

Plow the grooves for the panels in the frame pieces. This plow plane will take irons of different widths and has stops and fences to cut grooves of different depths and locations on the workpiece.

Scribe around all the pieces of the frame with a morticing gauge. Always gauge from the face side on all pieces.

*Mark the tenon shoulders by cutting
with the scribing knife held against the
blade of the try square. Then slice a
groove with a chisel, tilting it toward the
waste that will be removed in cutting the
tenon.*

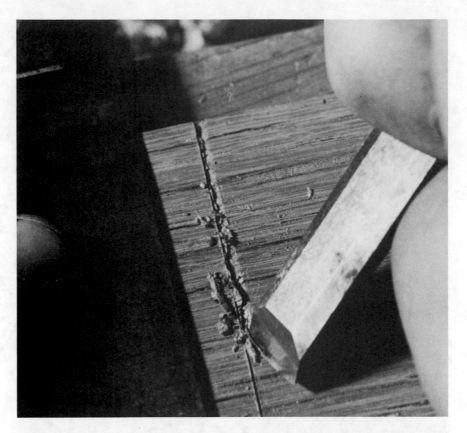

*Set the saw in this groove and saw down
to the line scribed with the morticing
gauge.*

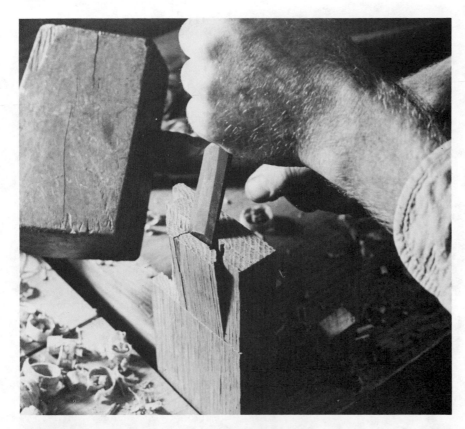

If the grain is straight, you can split away the cheeks of the tenon.

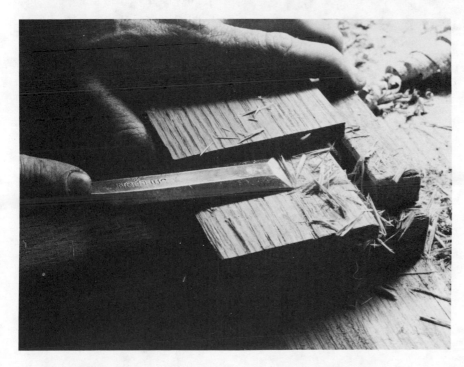

Shave the tenon smooth with a bench chisel held flat.

Morticing

Haunching. The pieces removed from the rail tenons will allow the ends of the mortices in the stile to remain closed. The actual haunch is the piece that is left to extend into the groove in the stile.

Set the prepared rail tenon on the face of the stile where the mortice will go. See that it is properly positioned and scribe the dimensions of the tenon onto the stile.

Lead these lines around the stile with a try square. Morticing can be done with any sort of chisel, but the thick morticing chisels are certainly best. The expression for this job is "chopping mortices." If you have ever been in a cabinet shop while several people were doing this at once, you know what I'm talking about; the whole building shakes under the pounding. This battering can easily break out the end of the mortice, ruining the stile. For this reason, you should leave the stiles longer than their final length, with an extra inch of wood on each end to add the strength needed to withstand the rigors of morticing. After the frame has been driven together (this can damage the mortices too), you can cut the stiles to length.

Start the mortice by setting the flat side of the chisel at one end of the scribed mortice, well inside the scribed end line. You want to cut out the middle of the mortice first and then square up the ends. Drive the chisel straight in with a single blow. The angle of the bevel will carry it toward the line a bit. Move the chisel slightly along the mortice and drive it in again. Continue doing this until you get near the far end. Now turn the chisel around and head back the other way. Each blow of the mallet will drive the chisel in only 1/2 inch at most, but heading back and forth, taking more on each pass, gets you through in no time. When you have reached the proper depth (if you're cutting all the way through the stile, go halfway from one side and halfway from the other), square up the ends

Haunching

Once the basic tenon has been cut, you must cut part of it away to allow the ends of the mortices in the stiles to remain closed. This is done only on the four corner joints, of course, not on any intermediate rails or mullions. I usually cut away a portion about equal to the thickness of the rail. Since I cut the mortice to match the tenon (the reverse of the standard procedure), I seldom measure this.

It is important when you cut away part of the tenon to leave a stub, or "haunch," remaining, rather than cut clean up to the tenon shoulder. For one, you want to fill the gap in the end of the stile that is left from plowing the groove. Second, even if there were no groove in the stile, you would want to create a short one to take the haunch for the strength this adds to the joint.

Scribe the dimensions of the rail tenon onto the stile. The inch of extra wood to the left will strengthen the stile during morticing and assembly, after which the stile will be cut off flush.

Chop the mortice halfway through from one side.

Then finish up by chopping the rest of the way from the other side.

down the back side so that all the edges will fit into the grooves. Make the panel wide enough that its long-grain sides will sit halfway down in their grooves. Remember that the panels must be free to move around, so don't defeat this by gluing them into their grooves.

Drawboring

The assembly process is fairly straightforward; you simply put the frame together around the panels. Use glue to hold the mortice and tenon joints together and reinforce them with pegging that uses the time-honored technique of offsetting the peg holes, or "drawboring."

To drawbore a joint, first bore the peg holes through the mortice in the stile before you try to fit the tenon in. Clean up the inside of the mortice with a broad, thin paring chisel and make any necessary adjustments to get a snug fit. Put the tenon into the mortice and drive the joint up tight.

Take the same auger and push it back into the peg holes to mark the tenon where the auger would have passed through it if it had been in place when the first holes were bored. Separate the joint and find this mark on the tenon. Now, move over "about the thickness of a shilling" (1/16 inch) *toward the shoulders of the tenon* and bore on through with the same auger.

Spread glue on the cheeks of the tenon and inside the mortice and reassemble the joint. Drive a tapered peg through the offset holes and the joint will pull up tight. Check for squareness before the glue dries.

Now that you have a door, all you need is a house to go with it.

of the mortice with the flat of the chisel against the end grain.

The Panels

You can show off your best wood in the panels. The stiles and rails frame it just as you would a fine painting. The basic panel can be no more than an expanse of wood, tapered around the edges to fit into the grooves plowed in the frame. The more usual treatment, however, is to define a central raised area by a distinct shoulder, away from which the edges taper down to fit into the grooves. This process is called "panel raising," and there are special planes

by the same name that do the job. Some of these planes have vertical cutters, or "snickers," that precede the plane iron to slice the cross grain of the top and bottom of the panels. Lacking this feature, other planes require you to precede the cross-grain cut with a "cutting gauge," essentially a marking gauge with a knife blade instead of a scribe.

If you don't have a panel-raising plane, you can still find many ways to accomplish the same task. You can use a plow plane to make a groove all the way around the raised area that is wide enough to let you use one of your regular planes. You can also do the whole job with a regular rabbet plane.

After raising the panel, taper

Raising a panel means planing away around the sides. The cross grain at the top and bottom of the panel must be severed with a cutting gauge to ensure a smooth shoulder without splintering.

This panel-raising plane has a skewed iron to cut cross grain smoothly.

The right plane makes it easy.

You can also raise a panel by plowing a groove around it that is wide enough to allow a regular bench plane to engage the wood. The rabbet plane at left can cut up to a square shoulder without the aid of the plow plane.

 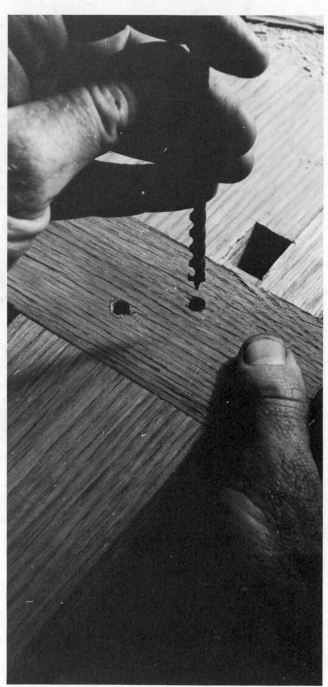

To drawbore a mortice and tenon joint, first bore the peg holes through both cheeks of the mortice.

Assemble the joint as tightly as possible and push the auger into the peg holes to make marks on the tenon.

Disassemble the joint and bore the peg holes through the tenon, offset toward the tenon shoulder from the marks.

Driving in the tapered pegs will draw the joint up tight.

The haunch on the rail fills the groove in the top of the stile.

Chapter 14. Log Houses

There is no building which fits so naturally in a wild landscape as a good, old-fashioned log cabin. It looks as if it really belonged there.
—D. C. Beard, *Shelters, Shacks and Shanties* (1914)

Nothing is more evocative of the American experience than the rugged simplicity of the log house. A Scandinavian form, log buildings were quickly adopted by immigrants from other countries; they spread throughout the country in the eighteenth and nineteenth centuries. Log houses were well adapted to the time and place of early America. They could be built with little more than an axe, a good eye, and common sense. The thick log walls would stop a bullet as well as the winter cold, and they provided a use for all those trees that had been felled to clear the land.

Everyone is familiar with the archetypal log cabin of round logs with saddle-notch corners and smoke that always seems to be curling up from the chimney. Self-conscious American popular culture has taken pride in this image since the 1840s when the "log cabin and hard cider" campaign of presidential candidate William Henry Harrison adopted this form of construction as a symbol of honest virtue.

Although the standard image of the log cabin has round logs with the ends hanging out, most log homes of the nineteenth century, especially the better ones that have survived, were built with logs that had been flattened on two sides to produce even, rather than corrugated, walls. Many, if not most, of them were built with the intention of covering over the logs with weatherboards as soon as the walls were up. When everybody lived in log houses, it wasn't something to flaunt.

Rather than try to deal with all aspects of log construction here, I'll look in detail at the processes of hewing, or squaring, the logs and cutting the most commonly found corner joints, the V-notch and the half-dovetail notch.

If you are intent on building a log house, first go out and cut and square the four bottom logs and move them to the building site. Doing this, you can make sure that you haven't planned on a bigger building than you can handle. Moving and squaring these first four logs will give you an idea of how much will be involved: just multiply the labor expended on these first four logs ten to thirty times, depending on the height of the building and the size of the logs. Without using heavy power equipment, you will find 22-foot logs about all you, your horse, and your friends will want to handle. Green timber of this size can weigh as much as a small car, so be reasonable.

Logs

Logs for building with must be straight and tall with slow, even tapers and no large branches. Poplar, aspen, pine, and other softwoods are best suited to the purpose today. Earlier times had more interesting choices in materials. I once directed the reconstruction of an 18-by-22-foot story-and-a-half log house built in the 1830s in central Illinois that was constructed almost entirely of walnut and chestnut. These may have been all that they had to work with. The uppermost logs of the building, the top plates, were 9-by-18-inch, 22-foot-long walnut timbers. Those were the days.

Remember that wood is much easier to work when it's green, but weighs about half as much when it's dry. With this in mind you may want to do most of your squaring axe work in the woods, which will lighten the load considerably and alleviate the need to clean up the piles of chips that would otherwise accumulate at the building site. A sound procedure is to fell a tree, cut it to length (plus a foot or so extra), and then remove the bark. Taking the bark off will clear the surface of the log for marking out the guidelines for hewing, as shown later, and needs to be done anyway to protect the log from insect attack. If you are cutting in the spring or early summer, most of the bark will come off in one big piece, which can then be used as temporary roofing. Make a slit down one side and use a stick, sharpened to a blunt chisel point, as a barking spud to ease off the bark.

Lining Out

It's not difficult to square up a log by eye without using guidelines for the axe work. I often use this method when I'm doing the initial squaring off in the woods. However, when precision is important, taking the time to line out the work will save time later on.

The problem is to define a level plane on two sides of an irregular cylinder. If the log were small enough to hold in one hand, you could define a perfect plane surface on one side of it by dipping it partway into a still pond and then cutting off all of the wood in the wet area. Repeating the process equidistant from that surface would give you a completed cabin log. You can get the same effect by tracing either level or plumb lines on both ends of the log and then connecting them along the length of the log with lines created by popping a snap line against the side. Gravity is the same at both ends of the log, so you can be sure that everything will come out perfectly flat as long as the log does

It's easy to square up a log by eye in the woods. Chop in a notch every foot or so and then pop out the chunks in between them.

More careful work can be laid out with snap lines. Use a plumbline or level to mark both ends of the log.

Be sure to snap the line in the same plane that you want to define. Here, horizontally for a horizontal surface.

not move before you get both ends marked. When you are hewing a lot of logs to the same thickness, usually 6 to 8 inches, save time by using a plumb bob hanging across a board that is as wide as you want the logs to be.

Once both ends of the log have been scribed, prepare your line by running it through whatever marking medium you have at hand. Pokeberry juice or charcoal and water leave the clearest lines. The line must be pulled tight between the two points and then pulled out and snapped in the same plane as the surface that is to be removed. Snapping the line in the proper plane is very important, for the irregularities in the log will throw your line off if you're not careful.

Hewing

Hewing, loosely speaking, refers to the shaping of some material by the repeated blows of a sharp instrument. When we talk about hewing logs, we usually mean two processes. The first is the "scoring," which roughly removes the bulk of the wood. Then the remainder is sliced off with a special axe to leave a smooth and level surface.

There are several ways to proceed with the preliminary axe work now that the log has been marked out. If you have a lot of wood to remove from the sides (say 4 or more inches), one fast way to work is to stand on the log with the side to be hewn facing out and use the felling axe to chop in notches every foot or so down to the line. You can then remove the bulk of the wood by splitting off the chunks between the notches. This is the method most old folks remember, as millions of railroad ties were cut in this manner.

When there are only 2 or 3 inches of wood to remove, popping off chunks from a horizontal face is fast and accurate.

Finish the surface by slicing down across the grain with the broad axe.

Another technique that I use more often on smaller logs is to set the log on 2-foot-high benches with the surface to be flattened turned up. Then, standing alongside the log, I chop down with the felling axe to remove a chunk every 4 inches or so. If you are right-handed, you will progress from the left end of the log to the right end, moving from the cut area into the uncut. The point is that each piece must be free to fly off to the left as your axe enters the wood from the right. Lefties simply reverse the directions and proceed in their usual manner. This technique is quite accurate and most efficient when you're cutting off 3 inches or less.

All of this hitting the log with the axe tends to move it about in unwanted directions. The most familiar method for holding the logs steady is to use a giant staple, called a spike dog (see chapter 11), which you drive into the log and the supporting cross log or bench. Another method, and one which I use most often, uses flats cut with the axe on the underside of the log where it rests on the benches.

Having removed the bulk of the material with the felling axe, you will need the broad axe to complete the job. The short handle canted out to the side and the single-beveled cutting edge allow you to work down the log across the grain in a shearing cut. Broad axes, big as they usually are, are finishing tools. The fifteenth-century poem "The Debate of the Carpenters Tools" had this to say about the broad axe:

> The brode axe seyd withouten mysse,
> He seyd: the pleyn my brother is;
> We two schall clence and make full pleyne.
> That no man schall us geyne-seyne,

Leave the sills (the bottom logs of the walls) round and protruding on their *inside faces to support the floor and the floor joists. Hang the joists from mortices* *cut in the sills and then adz them level.*

And gete oure mayster in a yere
More sylver than a man may
   bere.

In the scoring process, the felling axe removes pieces of wood in chunks; the broad axe removes flakes or sheets of wood. Set the log so that the rough surface to be hewn is vertical and, starting at the left end with a right-handed axe, make one quick pass as you walk forward beside the log with a slightly circular, slicing cut across the grain to bring the surface down so that your hands will clear. Then, come back down the log with a finer cut that removes the score marks down to the line. If you hew with the log low to the

ground, you must be sure to keep the edge of the axe from going into the dirt. Having the log up on benches will not only protect the axe from being dulled but will protect you from backache as well.

Sills

Log houses have only two real sills, the bottom logs on the long sides of the house. Unlike the rest of the logs, which are hewn on two faces, the sill logs are hewn on three sides—top, outside, and bottom. The inside face is left rounded, as it needs to protrude in and support the

joists and flooring. These are the heaviest logs of the building and are the ones that you should prepare and move to the site before you set the foundations.

The sill logs support and tie together the entire building. Since they are closest to the ground, they are also the ones most prone to damage from termites and decay. No matter what sort of timber you plan to use for the rest of the building, the bottom logs are best hewn from the timber of the most resistant species that you can find. Our old friend the white oak is most often used where I live.

The ground-floor joists may be round logs hung from open mortices cut in the protruding insides of the sills. Once they are in place, you can bring them level by snapping lines along them from sill to sill and then hewing them off level with axe and adz.

Foundations

With at least the first four logs ready on location, you can begin the foundations. These usually consist of a fieldstone pillar at each corner of the building. The further north you go, the lower the house should sit; in the South, it should be set high, at least 18 inches. In the mountains, you will end up doing both at once.

The 3-4-5 method, a time-tested reduction of Pythagoras's theorem, is a handy and accurate way to locate the corner pillars and see that the building is square. Measure out from a corner along one side a distance of 3 units—axe handles, cubits, or whatever; then measure out along the other side a distance of 4 units. When the diagonal distance, the length of the hypotenuse, between these two points is 5 units, the corner is 90°. As a final check, when the bottom set of logs is in place, the two diagonals of this rectangular building should be equal in length. If they are not, make them so.

The foundations can be leveled by setting the hewn sills in place and then placing a spirit level on them. You can also use a length of hose to siphon inky water between two clear jugs placed at opposite ends of a log. The latter method is absolutely accurate, as the water will always seek its own level in both jugs.

Notching

The two great enemies of wooden buildings are fire and fungi. While water puts out fire, it also causes the greatest damage to buildings by promoting the growth of wood-destroying fungi. There is nothing wrong with wood getting wet as long as it can dry out rather fast. Decay begins when water gets into spots where it can't dry quickly, enabling the fungus to begin its patient work. One of the primary exposed tight spots on a log house is the corner joints, or notches. If rain running down the corner of a building encounters notches that are ill de-signed or badly cut, water will run down inside them and cause the corner to rot. Here again, under-standing the behavior of the material determines good design. A long-lasting log joint must shed water.

The two corner joints that are most used in my part of the country are the V-notch and the half-dovetail notch. They are both easy to do and shed water quite well. To ensure a strong, tight fit the top half of each joint is custom cut to match the already cut bottom half. The top half can be made to fit the bottom half using any of several tools—such as dividers, patterns, or a framing square or other straight edge—to transfer the dimensions of the bot-tom cut to the top. The method that I use most often and the one that I have detailed here employs the framing square.

No matter what kind of joints you are cutting, don't cut the log to the precise length of the wall until after you have completed cutting the notches. Once the joint is done and the log is down in place, you can cut off the excess to leave a square corner. Cutting the upper log to length before you start notching

can result in the embarrassment of knocking the whole end of the notch off with a single misdirected blow.

The V Notch

To begin laying out a V-notch joint, set the log up on the building where it is to go. Reach behind this log and mark its thickness on the two log ends that it is sitting on. These marks tell you how far back on the end logs to cut the lower parts of the joints. Now, roll the top log back out of the way and cut the seats on both of the bottom logs. You can do this by eye with just a hand axe. Chop away on both sides of the log to leave a ridge down its center. The two side slopes should make an angle with one another of from 90° to 120°. The narrower the angle, the more fragile the upper half of the joint will be.

When both of the lower logs have been properly shaped, roll the top log back into place. Before you do anything further, measure the distance between this log and the one below it on the same side to see how far down the top log needs to sink in order to close up the gap between them. This is how deep you can make the notches in the upper log before the gap is completely closed.

To transfer the dimensions of the seats that you have cut on the lower logs onto the upper log, leave the log sitting right where it will go and find a framing square or some-thing with two parallel straight edges. Hold one blade of the square with the lower edge sitting flat on one of the two slopes cut on top of the lower log. Now scratch or make a pencil line on the top log along the upper edge of the square. Repeat this by setting the square on the other slope, and the two lines will

V notches shed water well.

*Set the log into place and scribe its
thickness on the log beneath it.*

Roll the log back out of the way and chop a V on the lower log, using the scribed line as the inner limit.

intersect, forming the apex of the V notch. Add on parallel lines to this upside-down V until you reach the depth that you want the upper log to sink down to. Do the same thing on the back face of the log and to the other end and you have the outline of the notches.

Roll the log back away again so that the notches face up and have at it with your axe. When you have chopped out down to the line, roll the log back into place and see how it fits. Make any necessary adjustments, cut the excess off the ends, and move to the next log.

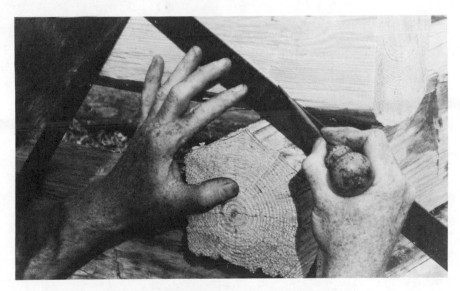

Roll the top log back into place and transfer the shape of the V up onto it by setting the square (or anything with parallel sides) on the slopes of the lower log.

Transfer both slopes of the V and then add parallel lines until the depth of the notch will be equal to the distance that you want the top log to sink to close the gap.

Do the same thing on the back side of the log.

Roll the log over again and chop down to the scribed lines.

Drop the log back into place and check the fit.

The half-dovetail notches always slope down across the grain of the lower log to the outside.

Half Dovetails

Believe it or not, half-dovetail notches are even simpler to cut; they just look harder. The process is the same as for the V notches, except that you cut just one slope on the logs instead of two. You won't get confused if you always think of sloping down to the outside, across the grain of the lower logs. It is this outward-facing slope that sheds the killer rain.

When you transfer the shape of the half-dovetail slope onto the upper log, you use essentially the same process that you used for the V notch. The only difference is that the inner limit of the upper half of the joint is determined by holding the square flat against the inside surface of the lower log, meaning, straight up and down.

Finishing Up

To complete the log house, continue adding logs until you arrive at one that will be over the uppermost log that has to be cut for a window, door or fireplace opening. When you have this log notched in place, roll it back out of the way and cut the length of the opening through only the uppermost log. This will give you a space to fit in the crosscut saw to finish the rest of the opening once the rest of the logs are in place. To keep the logs around a door or window opening from falling down as you cut them, spike a temporary plank to the face of all the logs on both sides of the opening. Once you have finished cutting the opening, you can case it with an interior frame through which you bore a hole and peg into the end grain of each log.

Second-floor joists can also be round and flattened only on the upper side, or they can be finished to suit the character of the building. The dimensions of the joists must be appropriate for the span, the load, and the spacing between them. Remember that doubling the breadth of a joist doubles its stiffness, but doubling its depth quadruples it. They are set into notches cut through the long-side logs. These notches should be cut when you get to their level in laying up the building, when you can get to them easily.

Give the rafters a good steep pitch, at least 45°, if you're going to put on a shake roof. The rafters can be full round poles, joined with pegged half laps at the top and notched into the plate.

The stuff that you put between the logs to close up the cracks has two components—the chinking and the daubing. The chinking is the split saplings, rocks, or whatever, that you jam in between the logs to make the cracks small enough that the daubing (mud or mortar) can seal it all up. Your daubing should be a soft material rather than a hard cement that won't give with the movement of the logs. I mix up various concoctions of clay, lime, and straw and resign myself to annual maintenance duty. Be sure to undercut the daubing in such a way that it won't collect and trap rainwater running down the outside of the logs.

Have a party when you're done.

Cut the slope on the bottom log, transfer the dimensions with the square, and chop the upper notch.

The pegged frame of a fireplace opening on a log house being reconstructed. Pockets cut through the wall to carry the second-floor joists are visible in the upper left.

Pole rafters, half lapped and pegged at the ridge.

Notches cut in the uppermost log or plate hold the bird's-mouthed rafters.

Chapter 15. Timber-Frame Construction

His delight was the construction of timber-framed farm
buildings; it was work which, somehow, suited his disposition.
—Walter Rose, *The Village Carpenter* (1937)

We often look at old buildings and marvel that they were built so well to have lasted so long. From this we tend to generalize about how well "they" used to build things back then. But a kind of natural selection has been at work here to ensure that only the fittest buildings have survived. We are left with only the finest work to judge our ancestors by. The bad work is compost.

The old survivors are the best teachers. This is not say that you can't learn from failures as well; the best and the worst have much to show you. Old buildings can show you what has worked and what has not worked in your neck of the woods. You can look at a joint that has failed and see why it has failed.

This looking at joints and timbers is something that people began to do in a different way in the eighteenth and nineteenth centuries. After countless generations of reliance on tradition and custom, builders began to apply the scientific method of experiment and analysis to the principles of carpentry. People began testing the breaking strength and resistance to shear of different sorts of timber, testing it across the grain, along the grain, in beams, as columns. From these experiments they began to formulate builders' manuals that would enable anyone who could afford the price of the book to design the strongest possible joints and consequently buildings.

For a simple example of the application of these principles, look at the joint that connects the top of a single upright post with the end of a horizontal timber. This joint consists of a tenon cut on the top of the post and a mortice cut into a horizontal beam near its end. The object of the joint is to prevent the beam from pulling back off the post, so it can fail in two ways: the end of the mortice in the beam can break out along the

grain, or the tenon on the post can shear off across the grain.

Since either one of these failures could bring a roof down around our ears, we have a strong incentive to do all that we can to maximize the strength of both areas. Without changing the dimensions or positions of the two timbers, all we have to work with are the relative proportions of the two elements of the joint.

Wood shears more easily along

One of two things must happen for this beam to pull off of the post. Either the tenon on the post must fail and shear off across the grain, or the end of the mortice on the beam must break out in two long-grain shear failures. Pegs add strength and complicate calculations. All factors must be carefully balanced—for failure will occur at the weakest point.

Inky water siphoned between two milk jugs will seek its own level. The half-lapped corners of the sills will be locked together by the long tenon on the bottom of the corner post.

the grain than it does across the grain, so it stands to reason that the long-grain area of the end of the mortice in the beam should be made greater than the cross-grain area of the tenon. To continue our example, since experiments have shown the strength of the cross grain per square inch in the species of pine that we are using to be about eight times that of the long grain, we need to make the danger area of the mortice eight times larger than that of the tenon. This disproportioning of surface area gives us equal proportions of strength in the mortice and the tenon, and the joint is as strong as it can be.

However, when the effects of pegs, cutting errors, unseasoned wood, and knots and checks are added to our example, book learning goes out the window. On paper, seasoned yellow pine has a safe long-grain shear resistance of 125 pounds per square inch and 1000 pounds per square inch across the grain. Oak has 200 pounds per square inch along the grain and the same as pine across the

grain. This is a helpful exercise, but no substitute for being there. I have to see the wood and the cut of the joint to tell what is right, and I can tell what is right, what will and will not work, because I have seen the test of time in the old buildings around me. Beyond all of the reading that you need to do before you attempt any timber framing, you really should go out and see for yourself what worked for your trees, your winds, your termites, and your ancestors in your part of the country.

Building the Shop

We built the shop along the lines of some of the surviving ante-bellum farm buildings in the area. Using salvaged timbers saved a lot of money, but limited the choice of dimensions. Everyone helped through the coldest winter in years to finish the shop so that I could be open by early spring.

We began in mid-October by

laying the 4-by-8-inch oak sills on stone foundations. The 4-inch thickness of the salvaged timbers was not enough to allow for more secure bridle joints at the corners, so we used half laps. Later, the long tenons on the bottoms of the corner posts would pass down through these half laps and lock the corners together.

Once the sills were down and level, we began the preparation of the wall components in yellow pine —corner posts, studs, angle braces, and top plates. When these were all ready, we could proceed to assemble the wall on the ground, peg the mortice and tenon joints up tight, and then raise the wall up into place.

Corner Posts

The corner posts were 6-by-6-inch timbers hewn to an L shape so that their inside corners didn't protrude into the interior of the building. In some old houses, these L-hewn corner posts were often as much as

Hewing the corner post to an L shape. Following this initial shaping, the rest of the wood will be removed by chopping in along the grain.

20 inches on a side. They were cut to this shape by chopping in along the grain with an axe, just as in the initial hollowing process for dough bowls. The tenon on the bottom to go through the sills where they intersected in the corner was a simple 2-by-2-inch extension left in the center of the 6 by 6. On the top, however, this corner post had to support and hold the two narrow top plates of the two intersecting walls. This called for a more complex joint with two tenons. We could have used a much bigger timber than a 6 by 6 for the corner posts, but this was all we had.

The two top plates intersect on top of the corner post. The L shape of the post keeps it from protruding into the room.

Studs

For studs we used 4 by 4s, tenoned on the top and bottom to go into the plate and sill. Since the sill was 8

Top view of the intersecting plates. The extra length of plate protruding to the left can now be sawed off. It was left on to strengthen the end of the mortice in the plate during the raising of the building.

A bucksaw for firewood cutting is the fastest way to saw a tenon shoulder.

inches wide, we had a lot of room to put in a mortice to take the tenon on the bottom of the stud. So here we were able to make a 2-inch-wide "side tenon" by cutting away half the thickness of the stud. This would not work on the top of the stud where it went into the 4-inch-wide plate, because the plate was no wider than the stud. Here we cut "central" tenons 1 1/2 inches wide.

To lay out the studs for cutting, we all used the same "story pole," cut to the exact length of the stud, from tenon shoulder to tenon shoulder. Then, to lay out the tenons (or mortices) we used framing squares. On rough timbers you have to use a framing square more like a surveyor's transit and sight along its length to correct by eye any bow or bumps in the timbers. Using it in the normal way assumes that you have a

perfectly straight, flat timber—a rare occurrence. When we laid out tenons (or mortices) in the middle of a timber, we just set the appropriate width limb (2 inches or 1 1/2 inches) of the square on the timber, lined it up by eye in what looked to be the center of the timber, and scribed down both sides. This "eyeballing" worked quite well for our purposes.

It's interesting that the 2-inch and 1 1/2-inch tenons and their corresponding mortices are the same width as the body and tongue of most framing squares. The old rule for proportioning the width of a mortice and tenon joint in equal-sized timbers is to make them between a third and a half of the width of the timbers involved. Any wider and the cheeks of the mortice would be too weak; narrower and the tenon would be too weak. In the

4-inch timbers that became standard in the later years of timber framing, this proportion comes to 1 1/2 inches. The widths of the square are templates for mortice and tenon layout in standard-dimension timbers. The tools and the work evolved together.

Once the tenons were laid out, we cut them across the grain with bucksaws and then split off the cheeks. Further smoothing was done with the framing chisels, held with the flat down, slicing across the grain.

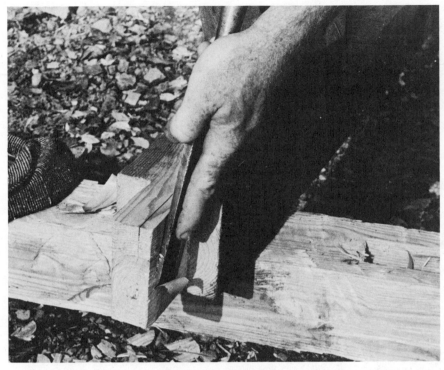

Shave the cheeks of the tenons with the framing chisel.

Morticing

With the posts, studs, and braces ready, the sill and the plate were laid alongside one another so that their mortices could be laid out at the same time. This is a good way to eliminate error and to ensure that all the studs will stand vertical. The widths of the mortices were 1 1/2 inches in the plate and 2 inches in the sill. We quickly scribed them with the aid of the framing square. The lengths of the mortices, however, were determined by the actual dimensions of the stud for each individual mortice. This varied from 3 7/8 inches to 4 1/8 inches, so every stud was laid down across where its mortice would go and scribed down on both sides.

Boring Machines

Some timber framers feel about their boring machines the way a violinst feels about his Stradivarius. A big T-handle auger can do the same job, and of course, you could do all the morticing with just a chisel, but a boring machine somehow makes it special. It's the right tool in the right place. These machines, with their cast gears and interchangeable parts, came along in the mid-nineteenth century and made the job of morticing easier and faster. To use it, sit or kneel on the base of the machine, which, in turn, sits on the timber to be morticed. The frame of the machine assures that the auger is penetrating at a right angle to the work or, in some adjustable models, at any angle set on the machine. The

two hand cranks allow the continuous turning of the auger bit, rather than the on-off changing of hand positions required with the T-handle auger. When you reach the right depth with the auger, back up a bit to disengage the lead screw, flip a lever to engage the rack and pinion, continue cranking forward, and the aguer climbs back up to the starting position. On some machines, the retraction of the auger was automatic with a preset depth stop. These wonderful machines are no longer manufactured, but I expect they'll be back one day.

Although the auger bits are interchangeable on boring machines, we used two machines to save time, one with a 1 1/2-inch auger and one with a 2-inch auger. The 2-by-4-inch mortices needed only two holes, the 1 1/2-by-4-inch mortices got three, with the middle hole saved until last.

The essential tools for cutting mortices are the mallet and chisel. Even holes started with a boring machine must be finished with a chisel. Boring machines are fun and practical to use, but they are not essential to the job. The same is true of corner chisels. They can give you a perfectly square corner very quickly, but so can the skillful use of a regular framing chisel.

Corner chisels are still being manufactured, but years ago when I was getting started, I couldn't find one anywhere. I was convinced that I had to have one, and finally resorted to forging one out of a section of angle iron from an old bed frame. I tried it and it worked, but it obviously wasn't going to hold up under heavy use. Not a day later, a friend came back from up north with a box full of corner chisels and sold me three of them. This seems to be axiomatic—going ahead with the work makes the tools show up. They also seem to come in threes. After

The boring machine makes morticing go quickly.

looking for years, I finally found a boring machine for sale at a price that I could afford. Within two weeks I found two more, even cheaper. Determination is a magnet.

Assembly—Drawboring and Pegging

Once everything was cut and morticed and tenoned, we began the task of putting the frames together on the ground before raising them into place. The raising process puts a lot of strain on the joints; in fact, this may be the most stress a building will suffer in its lifetime.

A properly designed building should stand firm without pegging the joints, but they do add stiffness. Where pegs were felt to be necessary, we used drawboring, the same technique used earlier to assemble the frame in our panel-frame door. In this method the peg holes are offset slightly through the mortice and the tenon, so that the joint will be drawn up tight by the action of the pegs.

We had a number of onlookers pass by as we worked, and each of them seemed to be privy to at least one of the secrets of old-time buildings. Two pervasive beliefs about what they used to do "back then" were repeated again and again. The first was that they always used oak or locust for pegs. I guess they didn't know that back then, because the surviving buildings from the eighteenth and nineteenth centuries in our region are all pegged with heart pine. The old first-growth pine was even stronger than the first-growth oak in resisting cross-grain shear. The other piece of advice we heard, although much more infrequently, was to use green, unseasoned pegs. Now even if you could drive in a

A corner chisel squares up the round holes.

Morticing the plate. Custom cut and test fit each joint on the ground if you can.

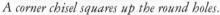

green peg without having it bend over, you know what would happen when it dried out.

So, thanking the "fence foremen" for their helpful hints, we went ahead and split 8-inch-long blocks of heart pine to rough square billets, left them in the sun for a few weeks, finished drying them by the fire, and sliced them with hewing hatchets to oversized octagonal pegs. The finished pegs were just a bit bigger than the 3/4-inch-diameter holes through which they were to be driven. They were left long and

slightly tapered and pointed on the end so that they would start in easy and drive up tight.

Although our pegs were a bit too small to qualify for the name, everyone called them "trunnels" (from tree nails). Even better, when we were shaving down pegs to their final size, we were practicing the ancient trade of the "mooter." Mooters were the workers who did the final shaping of the trunnels from the rough seasoned billets.

Mallets and Peg Driving

As always, we used wooden mallets to drive the pegs. The resilience of the wooden mallet head stores and releases the impact energy over a longer period of time. A metal hammer puts the energy into the peg so fast that much of the force of the blow is dissipated in distorting, rather than driving, the peg. When it's peg-pounding time, a wooden mallet will do more useful work than a steel hammer of equal weight.

Seating Angle Braces

Angle braces strengthen a building against the distortion of its right angles. This distortion can be a real problem when the roof is supporting thirty tons of snow and a forty-mile-an-hour wind is blowing. Using their compressive strength, the opposing pairs of braces in a wall keep it square by resisting the "closing up" of the corners. Angle braces in a building work in the same way that braces support a shelf on a wall.

The longer the spread of the braces, the more effective they are.

Braces can run from the post to the sill, from the post to the plate, or both. If you can do only one, bracing to the sturdier sill is more effective. We braced only to the plate, knowing that the 3-foot-high brick infill, or nogging, to be set into the lower

The layout of the brace tenon and shoulder. The lines at left and right are at 45° to the length of the brace. The line in the middle delineates the shoulder.

Sawing the tenon to length. The tenon shoulders have already been sawn and the cheeks chiseled off. The nose of the tenon has also been removed.

The brace mortice in this beam is fully housed or enclosed on the sides.

half of the walls would act as a brace to the sill.

Since a brace can be only as strong as its connection to the other timbers, this potential "weak link" must be made as strong as possible. The simple mortice and tenon is intended to hold two timbers together, not to support heavy transverse loads. A brace joint, or any other load-bearing joint, can be strengthened by adding a seat to the mortice to support the full width of the tenoned member. Accuracy of the cut is very important; it does little good to design a joint with 4 square inches of bearing surface if only 1 square inch actually makes contact.

Ready to go.

Together.

Brace measure tables are a common feature on most framing squares. On this century-old square, the length of the hypotenuse (brace) of the right triangle formed by a 48-inch run on both the post and the beam is given as 67.90 inches (.02 inches too much).

This brace is seated into the plate so that the tenon does not take the entire load.

The end wall ready to go up. Notice the tenons on the bottoms of the studs and corner post.

The rope tied at the top will keep the wall from being pushed clear over.

The 4-by-10-inch intermediate beam needed a tripod and block and tackle to get it up.

More help arrived for the big side wall.

Everything has to fit just right.

The big gable end rafters and collar beam move into place.

The intermediate rafters sit right on the plate.

Raising

Raising a timber-frame building is a magic moment. Weeks and months of hewing and sawing and boring and chiseling with nothing to show but a pile of numbered timbers culminate in just a few hours.

For a big barn raising, the whole community gathered to help out. At the start of the raising of a wall, or "bent," most everyone lined up along the top plate to await the command of the raising master. Others waited at the ends of long guy ropes and along the sill to ensure that none of the studs hung up in their mortices. When the command came, scores of hands lifted at once. The preparers of the traditional feast stopped to watch as the huge frame rose into the air. When the frame was up so high that the men along the plate could push no higher, some of them picked up pike poles to push with. As the frame went higher still, longer pikes were employed. Some of the crew rode the frame to help reset the long unwieldy pikes.

As each frame went up, the previously fitted and numbered connecting beams were driven into place and pegged. Each piece had to have been correctly cut; reputations were at stake. When the walls were all up, the crews raced to finish their allotments of rafters so that they could be first to be served at the long tables. In less restrained communities the evening would be full of dancing and drinking.

The modest walls of the shop hardly called for such a large crew, but the feeling was the same. We were able to grasp something that was good. That's the point of it— living the dream. The reality is yours forever.

Sources

Interest in traditional work ways is growing, and new books on the subject come out every year. Many of these new books are based on several primary works, and you owe it to yourself to read those books before you go on to the new ones.

The most comprehensive and valuable of the available sources are H. L. Edlin's *Woodland Crafts in Britain* (London: B. T. Batsford Ltd., 1949) and A. Viires's *Woodworking in Estonia* (Springfield, Va.: U.S. Department of Commerce Clearinghouse, 1960). These works demonstrate the enduring quality of a book written in succinct and scholarly style coupled with a genuine concern for the subject.

A very enjoyable and readable work, and one that has obviously had a great impact on me, is George Sturt's *Wheelwright's Shop* (Cambridge: Cambridge University Press, 1923). He knew this life and its worth, and his book is not just about making wheels.

Following close on Sturt is Walter Rose's 1937 work from the same publisher, *The Village Carpenter.* Rose also lived the life of the country craftsman and believed it worth preserving.

A paragon of straight-forward information on how to do things right is the 1923 edition of *Audel's Carpenters and Builders Guide*, in four volumes. You will have to look for these little black books in old-book stores, but they are well worth the extra effort. They were important in preserving the commonsense workmanlike approach to woodworking.

Readers familiar with the line-drawings in the secondary literature are often shocked to see the original photographs from which these were adapted in Henry Mercer's *Ancient Carpenter's Tools* (Bucks County Historical Society, Horizon Press, 1929). It's good to look at the foundations first.

Finally, there is a remarkably clever and useful volume available from the Early American Industries Association (c/o John Kebabian, 2 Winding Lane, Scarsdale, N.Y. 10583). After three centuries, Joseph Moxon's *Mechanick Exercises* (1703) remains a fresh and effective guide to blacksmithing, joinery, carpentry, and wood turning.

Along with the books are the museums. The people are there to help you and, given enough time, can provide a great deal of assistance. A visit to Colonial Williamsburg, Old Sturbridge Village, or any of the growing number of living history museums helps both you and those who have made the preservation of these skills their lifework.

I try to buy my tools mostly from junk and antique dealers, but several mail order houses carry traditional tools. Four familiar ones are: Woodcraft Supply Corp., 313 Montvale Avenue, Woburn, Mass.; Garrett Wade Co., 302 Fifth Avenue, New York, N.Y. 10001; Frog Tool Co., Ltd., Department P, 514 N. Franklin Street, Chicago, Ill., 60610; and Silvo Hardware Co., 2205 Richmond Street, Philadelphia, Pa. 19125.

Finally, a good group to get with if you are interested in tools and tradition is the Early American Industries Association. For information write: John S. Watson, Treasurer, Early American Industries Association, Post Office Box 2128, Empire State Plaza Station, Albany, N.Y. 12220.

Index

Numbers in italics refer to captions
   on those pages.